1900 House

MIND WHAT WINE IS TO THE BODY

BOOKS ARE TO THE

EX · LIBRIS

MACMILLAN

First published in 1999 by Channel 4 Books, an imprint of
Macmillan Publishers Ltd, 25 Eccleston Place, London SW1W 9NF,
Basingstoke and Oxford.

Associated companies throughout the world.

ISBN 0 7522 1711 9

Text © Mark McCrum and Matthew Sturgis, 1999
Diary extracts © The Bowler Family, 1999

The right of Mark McCrum and Matthew Sturgis to be identified
as the authors of this work has been asserted by them in
accordance with the Copyright, Designs and Patents Act 1988.

9 8 7 6 5 4 3 2 1

A CIP catalogue record for this book
is available from the British Library.

Design by Dan Newman/Perfect Bound Design
Special photography by Chris Ridley
© Chris Ridley/Channel 4/Channel 4 Books
Colour reproduction by Speedscan
Printed in England by Bath Press

This book accompanies the television series *1900 House*
made by Wall To Wall Television for Channel 4.
Executive producers: Leanne Klein and Alex Graham
Series producer: Simon Shaw

Contents

Introduction

The 1900 House experiment began life as a proposal for a television programme about domestic technology in the twentieth century – and how the numerous changes of the last hundred years have impacted on people's daily lives. As the editors and producers at Channel 4 and Wall To Wall Television discussed ways of dramatising and bringing alive these changes, the idea of involving a real family was floated.

It was a short step from there to deciding to set the whole experiment in a particular frozen moment of time. And what better moment than 1900: a hundred years before the upcoming millennium; the last year of the reign of Queen Victoria; the turning-point into the Century of Automation. It was a year that was still in living memory for a few; and yet, in technological terms, it was light years away.

Only a tiny minority of houses at that time even had electricity. For most, artificial light was provided by candles or incandescent gas 'mantles'; heat and hot water by the coal-fired 'range'. The telephone had been invented (in 1876), but was not in general use. There were few motor-cars. Transport was public – the railway, horse-drawn omnibus, in London the emerging Underground – with, for the wealthy, the option of horse-drawn hackney carriage or hansom cab. Not one item in the array of modern machinery we take for granted – fridges, televisions, videos – was even a gleam in the wildest inventor's eye.

Opposite: *The Bowler family of Somerset. Hilary, Kathryn, Joyce, Paul, Joe and Ruth were selected from over 400 applications.*

As the idea of trying to involve a real family took shape, the emphasis of the television series changed. The project would allow much more than just technological change to be examined. How would the family themselves respond? Would they draw closer and become more like our stereotypical idea of the Victorians? Would the father feel the need to take charge and become the 'master of the house'? Would the effort of cooking, cleaning and washing with old-fashioned devices and materials reduce the mother to an exhausted drudge? How would the children respond? From being a programme about inanimate devices, suddenly it was truly an experiment, which might have much to say about changes in family structure, attitudes, discipline and morals. 'We would be able to see,' said Simon Shaw, producer of the series, 'how dramatically every aspect of our lives has changed within a hundred years.'

Their ambition for the programmes, he felt, was to try to bring history alive in a tangible fashion. Viewers would be able to follow the family, who would 'smell, touch, taste and hear

what the period was actually like'. The plan was 'to take an everyday house, the sort that millions of us still live in, and see how life was for ordinary people'. By giving the family copies of the popular 'how to live' manuals of the period – from Cassell's *Book of the Household* to Mrs Beeton's famous cookbook – it would be possible to test the detail of late-Victorian life. Was it really necessary to have your front step brushed and cleaned by 7.30 each morning, as Mrs Beeton advises? Why was there so little mention of dustbins and waste disposal in Cassell's? And so on.

In addition, the experiment would provide a fascinating commentary on our own comparatively hi-tech, low-effort lives. What would the family miss most? The fridge? The car? The telephone? *Countdown*?

Now the search for an actual family began. From an initial response to newspaper adverts by 400 families, a shortlist of forty was drawn up. Interviews took place over a three-month period. Finally, after considering families whose chief breadwinner ranged from a policeman in Stoke-on-Trent to a health worker in Scotland, the Bowler family of Somerset were selected.

Paul, thirty-nine, the father, was a warrant officer with the Royal Marines at the Commando Training Centre at Lympstone, Devon; he had spent his entire adult life with the Marines, since joining up at the age of sixteen. Joyce, forty-four, the mother, was an under-eights adviser for Somerset Social Services, responsible for registering and inspecting daycare facilities. Having taken a B.Ed. in teacher training at Rolle College, Exmouth, in 1973–7, she had devoted her adult life to bringing up her five children and supporting Paul as he moved from post to post within the Marines. They had moved house 13 times in 16 years.

Paul and Joyce's eldest daughter Connie, nineteen, opted not to take part in the experiment; she would stay at home. So Kathryn, sixteen, studying law, English and the performing arts at sixth-form college, would become, in effect, the eldest daughter for the duration of the project. She would be joined by twins Ruth and Hilary, eleven, currently boarding at a military school, and only son Joseph, nine, a weekly boarder at Edington and Shapwick, a specialist school for dyslexics on the Somerset Levels. New schools were to be found for all of them in the Charlton area.

The family were thrilled to be chosen. Paul and Joyce had a longstanding interest in history and were regular visitors to National Trust houses. For Joyce the opportunity to get, as she put it, 'behind the guard-rail' and into living history was extremely exciting. She saw herself as a time-traveller and thought the project would be 'a wonderful adventure for the whole family'. (The 'being on TV' aspect of the experiment was not, she said, particularly an attraction.)

Paul was frank in admitting that he was doing the project for Joyce. 'She's followed me around for twenty-two years in the armed forces,' he said, 'and she's had to give up a teaching career to do that, and bring up our five children, so this is like a little "thank-you" for all the effort she's put in.'

The four children who had agreed to do the project shared their parents' enthusiasm. 'I was really excited and glad that we were chosen out of 400 and something amount of people,' said Ruth. 'I really didn't want to do it,' added Hilary, 'but when it came to the day of our interview I had really got the flow of it – I loved the idea.' 'All my friends are excited for me,' said Kathryn, 'and we've been joking about book signings.'

As the process of finding a suitable family had been going on, Wall To Wall's team had discovered a house suitable for complete conversion to the year 1900. It was in Charlton, south-east London, a district of the capital that had been built in the late-Victorian period to house the emerging 'lower middle class' of white-collar clerks and other professional support staff. Victorian expert Daru Rooke was brought in to oversee the transformation. As a social historian, he was intrigued by the idea of placing, as he put it, 'a modern family in a house of yesterday'. He was hoping that the three months would enable him 'to learn about the real details that we as historians have lost in only ninety-odd years. Publications and books of the period give you all the bigger things, but they will be finding out the detail, the real experience of life in 1900.'

In consultation with Daru, Simon Shaw and Wall To Wall drew up a strict set of rules for the family. There was little point, it was felt, doing the experiment unless the family agreed to give up the conveniences, appliances, luxuries and comestibles of the late twentieth century as completely as possible.

So: inside the house, everyone would wear period clothes at all times. Only food and drink typical of the period would be consumed, and all cooking would use the authentic equipment in the kitchen – modern machinery would be entirely banned.

Outside the house, every effort was to be made to minimise getting involved with a modern lifestyle. While travel on modern transport would be necessary to reach work (for Paul) or school (for the children) other 1999 activities would be restricted as much as possible. A packed lunch would remove the need to eat contemporary food. Telephone calls, it was agreed, should not be made, and again everyone would wear period clothes – except the children when they were at school. They would leave the house and change, by arrangement, at a neighbour's over the road.

The family would live on a strict budget, based on the typical expenditure of a Warrant Officer's family of the time. Foods could be bought at local stores, or ordered for delivery. A ledger would be kept, which Joyce would be expected to keep up to date. Each member of the family would be provided with a £20 note for emergencies.

Visitors would be welcome, especially if they wore appropriate period clothing, but they should not bring into the house any modern appliances or foods. Communications to the

Above: *Sixteen-year-old Kathryn Bowler. Initially she was enthusiastic about her Victorian clothes but quickly yearned for jeans and fleece.*

outside world should only be made via the 'postal service', which would, authentically, pick up and deliver three times a day.

Problems arising within the house should be resolved, in the first instance, by reference to the period manuals provided, in particular Cassell's *Book of the Household*. Should difficulties persist, a letter should be written to one of a selection of relevant experts, seeking his or her advice, which would be given, hopefully, by return of post. Training in the Victorian practices and techniques necessary to operate the house would be provided before the project started, in a preparation session at Shugborough Hall, a working Victorian stately home in Staffordshire.

Apart from visits by the film crew, the only twentieth-century equipment in the house would relate to health and safety. In the first instance, period medicines from the medical cabinet should be used. If any condition became more serious the local doctor should be consulted or the modern first aid-kit concealed in the larder should be used. Modern fire extinguishers and fire blankets would be provided for emergencies. The house would be equipped with comprehensive modern detection and alarm systems for heat, smoke, carbon monoxide and gas, as well as an intruder alarm. Finally, there would be two video-diary cameras concealed in the cupboards in the bedrooms, for family members to record their private thoughts.

With the rules agreed between the Bowlers and Wall To Wall, the stage was set for the three-month-long experiment. Each member of the family was given a diary, and it was hoped that these written accounts would supplement the individual reactions documented in the concealed video diaries.

In the twentieth-century comfort of their seventies-built semi-detached home, the Bowlers prepared for their great time-travel experiment, which was to begin on Sunday, 14 March 1999, just six short weeks after the family had been finally selected. How would they fare in their adventurous exploration behind the guard-rail of history?

Part One: The World in 1900

Late-Victorian Britain

In 1900, 50 Elliscombe Road was at the hub of things. It stood within a new suburb on the edge of the vast capital of a small island-nation that pulsed at the heart of a great empire, in a rapidly changing political and economic world. Each of these wider environments impinged in different but telling ways upon the life of number 50. In 1900 the house stood on the brink of a new century, one fraught not only with hope and possibility but also with doubt and even danger.

The world of 1900 was not the world of today. Much of that past context has, of course, vanished, and could not be readily recreated for the purposes of a TV programme. Re-establishing the British Empire is beyond even the resourcefulness of a TV documentary team. Nevertheless, for this book, it is worth sketching in some of the background, to give a broader sense of the pressures, prejudices and aspirations playing upon a middle-class suburban family of that time.

Some of the facts and some of the forces that marked life in 1900 do still persist today. An account of the social and political landscape of the period will reveal much that is surprisingly familiar, as well as much that is quaint and strange.

Britain, as the world's first great industrial power, had enjoyed an economic pre-eminence through much of the nineteenth century. By 1900, however, this position was being challenged – or had been overtaken – by the USA and Germany, by France and Russia. All these countries boasted decisive advantages of manpower and natural wealth. But British pride and self-confidence could seek comfort in the fact that Britain still maintained a place as the world's greatest trading and carrying nation. It was a position buttressed by the might of her Navy, which ensured that the seas were always kept open for the free traffic of free trade.

Free trade was the great motive force of world change during this period; and it is certainly familiar to us still. Since the 1850s successive British governments had promoted a policy of unrestricted trade between nations, trade free from tariff controls and protectionist exemptions, believing that this was the best way to ensure prosperity and promote progress. It was a policy that, by 1900, had laid the foundations for the so-called global economy, directed – in Scottish economist Adam Smith's memorable phrase – by 'the invisible hand of the market'.

Above: *The suburb of Charlton developed rapidly during the last years of the nineteenth century, on the land between Charlton House and the Thames.*

It is not too fanciful to suggest that this 'invisible hand' directed the construction of Elliscombe Road. In the 1880s the unrestricted influx of cheap wheat into Britain from the vast prairie provinces of North America, after several years of poor home harvests, decimated many traditional agricultural communities. British farms could not compete against the large-scale, mechanised production of the American farmers. This failure led to a mass exodus from rural areas into towns, as agricultural labourers sought new work and new opportunities.

Many gravitated towards London, swelling its numbers: by 1891 there were over four million people in the capital. The expanding population needed homes, and speculative builders were eager to provide them with housing. The development of Charlton – and of Elliscombe Road – was just part of this process.

At another, more intimate, level Britain's commitment to free trade would also have had an impact on the life that went on inside Number 50. Although the general, and desired, effect of free trade was to lower prices and improve the standard of living, only those with regular incomes could benefit. The instability of markets, the possibility of sudden and drastic shifts of fortune, bred a disquieting sense of impermanence. Ancient bonds and relationships were eroded. Jobs were not secure; incomes might not always be regular.

Change – abrupt, devastating and beyond the individual's control – became an expected factor of existence. In 1900, when social service provision was minimal and unfixed, this could be frightening. A select band of entrepreneurial spirits recognised the opportunities in such impermanence, but for the vast majority it created only a sense of anxiety. The anxiety was generally suppressed – or repressed – but it was telling. It stood behind the late-Victorian insistence on the outward forms of 'respectability': an attempt to create the illusion of stability in an unstable world.

Books of 1900

The Oxford Book of English Verse, *selected by Arthur Quiller Couch – a classic, and long-lived, anthology of English poetry; much quoted from by Rumpole of the Bailey.*
Lord Jim *by Joseph Conrad – a tragic yet ambiguous tale of Britain's far-flung trading outposts.*
The Wizard of Oz *by Frank L. Baum – the trip down the Yellow Brick Road began here.*
The Shadowy Waters *by W.B. Yeats – an attempt to combine Irish Nationalist sentiments with fashionable literary symbolism.*
The Interpretation of Dreams *by Sigmund Freud – a ground-breaking study of how dreams reveal an individual's subconscious fears and desires.*

Although Britain espoused the global market she also held a position as the head of a world empire. It was an empire that – with the notable exception of Australia – had been founded and expanded along the lines of trade. It played its part in the world economy, providing Britain with new materials, new markets, and a network of bases from which to carry on and police her trade. But, aside from its economic significance, the very fact of the empire lent a distinctive flavour to British life during this period.

Britons were proud of their empire, an empire upon which 'the sun never set'. It reached from Canada to Australia, from the Cape Colony in South Africa to the vast Indian subcontinent. It included Gibraltar and Hong Kong, Trinidad and Mauritius. And it was all held – in theory at least – under the stabilising influence of the *Pax Britannica*. Great Britain was, in its own estimation, the true heir of classical Rome.

Like Rome, Britain conferred cultural advantages on those it ruled. The empire was founded upon and sustained by a sense of moral superiority. It was the 'White Man's Burden' to civilise and govern his less fortunate brothers around the globe. Although the existence of the empire gave Britons an awareness, and even an experience, of the world's diversity and otherness, it also tended to reinforce a belief in the specialness of British institutions: justice, cricket, railway timetables and English itself. The English language was deemed to be one of the great agents of civilisation, the medium of Shakespeare, Milton and the Authorised Version of the Bible.

This pride in the benefits, and belief in the responsibilities, of empire pertained throughout the late-Victorian age. Although Britain did not, by and large, seek to extend its direct authority over its colonies at this time (the Commonwealth of Australia Act was passed in 1900) it continued to annex possessions around the globe. If anything, imperial concerns grew more marked towards the close of the century, as British superiority was threatened by internal insurrections and by the rival ambitions of Germany, France, Russia and others.

Throughout the period Britain was obliged to fight an almost continuous succession of colonial wars to reinforce and extend her power across Africa and throughout the East. In 1900 imperial pride and imperial anxiety were focused most keenly upon South Africa where the Boer War was in progress. The notion that a semi-irregular group of Dutch farmers could flout the might of imperial Britain was alarming. And the fact of British military incompetence in the prosecution of the campaign served to heighten the disquiet.

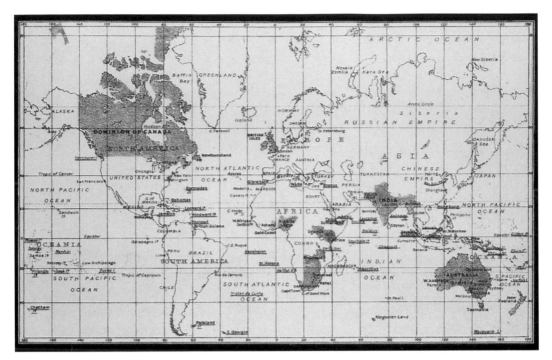

The pitch of this disquiet can be seen most clearly in the reaction against it: 1900 marked a rather illusory advance in British war-fortunes after the disasters of the previous year. Imperial troops, under Lord Roberts, began to impose the advantage of their numbers. When the besieged town of Mafeking was relieved by imperial forces, in May, Britain went almost mad with delight. There was dancing and revelry in the streets, and Mafeking Night was instituted, for years to come, as a popular celebration. To 'maffick' became a verb meaning to 'exult riotously'. It was around 1900 that patriotic pride first began to curdle into a less wholesome jingoism.

This trend, however, was only faintly perceptible at the time. The main focus for popular patriotic enthusiasm remained the Queen. Victoria had been on the throne for over sixty years (she succeeded in 1837). During that period

Inventions & Discoveries of 1900

The 'quantum theory' of energy was developed by the German physicist Max Planck.
The paperclip was invented by the Norwegian, Johann Waaler.
The Box Brownie instamatic camera was introduced by George Eastman.
Professor William Crookes seperates uranium.

she had transformed the monarchy from a sober, almost private, agency of national service into something approaching the flamboyant and demotic pageant that we know today. Her Diamond Jubilee celebrations of 1897 had given full scope for such stage-managed spectacle. The very fact of her longevity seemed like a national achievement.

There were other, more palpable, achievements to enjoy too. At home the year 1900 found Britain buoyed up on a thermal of prosperity. Real incomes had been increasing steadily over previous decades and the living conditions of most were improving. Universal suffrage was still several decades in the future, but the Reform Acts of 1867 and 1884 had greatly extended the

Above: *Mr Punch leading British and Imperial troops off to the Boer War. The progress of the war dominated the news in 1900.*

vote. The limited, Protestant, property-owning character of the old franchise had been dramatically altered by the admission of other denominations and other interests. The number of adult males eligible to vote had been increased from a mere twenty per cent to something over sixty. And the Education Act of 1870 had created a broader educated class eager to take up this political opportunity. Certainly the tenant of 50 Elliscombe Road, as a male, urban householder who paid rates, would have been brought within the new system.

The political landscape was gradually evolving into a recognisably modern one of mass parties and professionalised politicians. Kier Hardie, the Glasgow docker, was elected to the House of Commons in 1892, nominally as an Independent; and the following year the Independent Labour Party was founded. But the major reshaping of established political order during the previous decade and a half had been effected by the ever-vexatious 'Ulster Question'.

Above: *A souvenir of Victoria's Diamond Jubilee.*
She had raised the monarchy to a new level of popularity.

Above: *Regent Street at night in 1900. John Nash's original design was still preserved, but the aristocratic character of the shops was declining. Retailers were catering more to customers 'from the suburbs and country visitors'.*

Opposite: *Leicester Square was the heart of London's theatre-land. It was presided over by the statue of Shakespeare and the façade of the Empire Music Hall.*

The Liberal Party had been split by Gladstone's attempt to introduce a Home Rule Bill for Ireland in 1886. It never fully recovered. Gladstone's opponents within the party formed themselves into a new grouping, the 'Liberal Unionists', and henceforth allied themselves with the Tories. Together they enjoyed almost two decades of unbroken domination. In 1900 Lord Salisbury's Conservative ministry had been in power for five years.

Although there was little major legislation during this period, government – both central and local – was becoming increasingly active in many spheres of life. Government employment and government expenditure both increased dramatically during the last years of the century. By 1901 there were over 128,000 people employed in government service, an increase of thirty-seven per cent on the previous decade. New government departments proliferated: a Board of Trade in 1893, a Board of Agriculture in 1894 and a Board of Education in 1899. The London County Council was established in 1889, to provide a central elected body for the capital. And ten years later this measure was counter-balanced at a more local level by the London Government Act which created twenty-eight metropolitan borough councils.

If Britons became more thoroughly governed by their politicians, they also monitored their own lives more actively. Society became increasingly stratified by categories of class. Class

divisions became at once more marked and more significant. In political and economic terms the great divide was perhaps between the property-owning ruling class and the property-less industrialised working class. Both groups developed distinctive identities during the last decades of the nineteenth century. The former combined its increasingly City-based financial interests with a taste for conspicuous rural leisure – 'huntin', shootin', fishin'', and house parties. The latter forged a common culture from beer, sport and self-improvement.

> ## Plays Of 1900
>
> Herod *by Stephen Phillips – a very popular attempt to revive serious verse drama.*
> Mrs Dane's Defence *by Arthur Henry Jones – a play addressing women's issues.*
> A Midsummer Night's Dream, *lavishly produced by Herbert Beerbohm Tree, with live rabbits.*
> Mr and Mrs Daventry, *written by Frank Harris but based on a scenario provided by Oscar Wilde. (Wilde, it transpired, had sold the storyline not only to Harris but to several other interested parties.)*

Nevertheless it was in the area between these two classes that social gradations were perhaps most keenly noted and most fiercely patrolled. Nuances of etiquette, of language, of dress became all-important indicators of class status. Books and articles on 'modern manners' became popular for the uncertain and the aspiring. For, although the rungs of the class ladder may have become fixed, it was still possible to move between them. Rising incomes and the proliferation of white-collar jobs allowed many to climb from the 'upper working class' into the 'lower middle class' world so vividly recorded in *The Diary of a Nobody* and so lovingly recreated at 50 Elliscombe Road.

The great demographic change of the period – the shift of population from countryside to towns – has already been noted. Nowhere was this shift more marked than in London. At the beginning of the twentieth century there were some four and a half million people living in London, almost fourteen per cent of the entire population of England and Wales. The city had grown by more than half a million people since the beginning of the 1890s, and expansion seemed set to continue. The next largest cities – Liverpool and Manchester – had only something over half a million people each. In the face of this imbalance the provincial centres of mid-Victorian England began to wane. London drew more and more of the nation's populace, money and energy to its heart.

London drew people not only from all over the country but from all over the world, particularly from Europe. In the East End there was a large population of Russian and Polish Jews, fleeing from persecution. Surprisingly, perhaps, there were few non-Anglo

Above: *In 1900 there were 16,000 policemen in London and methods of detection were becoming steadily more scientific. The Central Finger Print Bureau was established in 1901.*

immigrants from around the empire, although they were – technically – free to settle, and would have received full citizenship had they done so.

The great expansion of London was achieved with remarkably little social cost. Extreme poverty and poor sanitation, although continuing facts in some areas, were being steadily eroded by increased employment and improving infrastructure. Flagrant prostitution in central London – most notably in the Strand and at the Leicester Square music halls – was a glaring ill to some, but in other respects the streets were remarkably safe. The crime rate had been declining steadily since the 1860s, despite the fact that both the number of crimes on the statute book and the number of police on the street were increasing. A regime of 'zero tolerance' seems to have been in operation: in 1900 you could receive a seven-day prison sentence for playing games in the street, using obscene language in public, sleeping rough or, even, riding a bicycle without lights.

London was developing into not just a great capital city but into a world metropolis. Following the defeat of France in the Franco–Prussian war of 1870–71 London had risen unchallenged as Europe's leading financial centre. The world's capital poured through London's banks and clearing-houses, and made money for those who handled it.

The money had to be spent and London became the seat of a newly emerging metropolitan culture of mass-consumption, served by mass-production and mass-retailing. Great London department stores began to rise up, offering the promise of choice and convenience. By 1900 Dickins & Jones had a staff of over 200, most of whom were was accommodated in a hall of residence nearby. Peter Jones, Liberty and – south of the river – Arding and Hobbs were all established. Although Harrods' current terracotta façade was not begun until 1901, the store itself was already boasting that it 'served the world'. In 1898 the first escalator in London was opened there. It is said that an assistant was designated to stand at the top of the flight

Top: *Department stores were becoming a feature of London life. The first escalator was opened at Harrods in 1898.*

Above: *Liberty & Co. Ltd, in Regent Street as it is today, specialised in selling goods from India, China and the Orient.*

Above and below: *Advertising in the press, and on hoardings, became increasingly prevalent, but also more subtle, at this time.*

It shines for all.

armed with a brandy flask and a bottle of sal volatile in order to revive startled customers.

Advances in printing technology – as well as the spread of literacy – led to a great proliferation of the popular press. Newspapers, magazines and weeklies clamoured for attention. And within their pages – as upon the walls and hoardings of the town – advertisements abounded. Many of the household brands of today first proclaimed themselves at this time: Lifebuoy soap, Coleman's mustard, Hovis, Bovril, Oxo, and Peak Frean biscuits. Others products of the time, such as Monkey Brand soap ('makes copper like gold, tin like silver, brass like mirror, crockery like marble, windows like crystal'), have been less enduring. Advertising became one of the dominant features of the age.

At one level this revolution replaced small-scale, hand-crafted diversity with large-scale, mass-produced uniformity. But, in fact, there were so many competing brands and products that choice tended to be increased rather than otherwise.

A similar trend occurred on the artistic front. Distinctive but limited regional forms of art began to be superseded by the spread of a world culture. German operas, French novels, Scandinavian dramas – each loudly promoted in the press – created a succession of 'booms' among London's cognoscenti. Traditional British forms of popular entertainment, such as the music hall, continued but they became increasingly elaborate and extreme in their effects. It was in the music hall that some of the early experiments with film were first shown.

Although artists were excited about some of the new opportunities opening up to them, they were also haunted by a sense of incipient decline – or 'decadence'. The world seemed weary. The great certainties and achievements of the High Victorian Age appeared to have passed. This sense of *fin-de-siècle* exhaustion pervaded, in different ways, the work of many home-grown writers of the period: it suffused the self-conscious weariness of such avowedly decadent figures as Oscar Wilde, Ernest Dowson and Arthur Symons. It also found vent in works of a very different stamp: the problem plays of Arthur Wing Pinero and George Bernard Shaw, the imperial novels of Joseph Conrad and Rudyard Kipling, the realism of Arnold Bennett and the science fiction experiments of H.G. Wells.

Above: *By 1900 Joseph Conrad (1857–1924), the Polish-born novelist, was emerging as a major talent with his dark tales of the sea and of human corruptability.*

Nevertheless, against this sense of exhaustion and decline ran another current of thought, more vital and optimistic. There was a widely held belief that the age was distinctively and uniquely 'modern'. Of course all ages are modern in their day, but the men and women of 1900 held a novel sense of the period's special 'modernity', its separateness from what had gone before, a belief that they were living in an era of new relations, new opportunities and new conditions. New technologies, new ideas, new social alignments seemed to crowd in upon the scene.

Indeed the very term 'new' became one of the ubiquitous features of the period. It was applied to everything: morality, humour, women, art, poetry, drama, and a raft of other contemporary phenomena. *Punch* eventually lost patience with this habit, and lambasted everything as 'the New Newness', complaining that the term had become a 'new-sance'. It was even suggested that the adage should be amended to, 'There's nothing old under the sun.'

This sense of newness and modernity was felt most keenly in London. New technologies were transforming the life and look of the capital: electric street-lighting, electric traction, telephonic communication were gradually superseding older modes and practices. The first motor-cars were seen on the streets. In 1896 the speed limit for 'horseless carriages' was tripled from four to twelve miles per hour.

As far as Victorians were concerned the Age of Speed had arrived. Indeed it seemed as if the whole metropolis now pulsed to a new rhythm – faster and more frenetic. The ancient progression of the seasonal cycle seemed almost obliterated by the artificial whirl of urban life. It

Above: *A caricature of the popular playwright Arthur Wing Pinero by the artist and theatre critic Max Beerbohm.*

Musical Debuts of 1900

Puccini's opera, Tosca, *was performed for the first time at Rome, in January.*
Debussy's Nocturnes *received their first performance in Paris in December.*
Edward Elgar's The Dream of Gerontius *was performed for the first time at the Birmingham Festival.*
Samuel Coleridge-Taylor's Scenes from the Song of Hiawatha *was praised as a work of 'the highest promise'.*

has been suggested that, to make good this deficiency, the new calendar of sporting mass-entertainment evolved. The football and cricket seasons provided urban man with an artificial cycle of his own.

As London life span ever faster, London itself – as if by centrifugal force – grew ever bigger. Throughout the late 1890s and early 1900s it spread 'fungus-like' in all directions. The new office-workers, required by London's thriving financial-services industry, needed accomodation. The spread and improvement of London's transport network ensured that this accomodation could be constructed further from the centres of work. The great shift in London's population during this period was away from the central boroughs and towards the newly constructed suburbs of the periphery.

Charlton was rapidly being transformed from a rural village, with its Jacobean manor house and parish church, into a trim red-brick suburb. By 1912, when the Survey of London recorded the area, there were only a few fields remaining: 'Between Victoria Road and Church Lane building is being rapidly pushed on, and the ground will soon be crowded with the exception of one very deep "coombe", full of trees, east of Elliscombe Road.'

Charlton, like much of south London, was well served by the existing railway network, which connected it with Cannon Street in the City, and Charing Cross in the West End. Indeed part of its route included the oldest stretch of railway in the metropolis: the line between Greenwich and London Bridge was begun in 1833. But it was the technological development of 'electric traction' at the very end of the 1880s, and the greater availability of cheap electricity during the 90s, that revolutionised London's transport – and London suburbia.

Most of London's rail-lines were electrified during this period, producing a faster, cleaner and more efficient service. Steam engines, though good over long distances, were unsuited to the stop–start conditions of local transport. Amalgamations of the various railway companies also contributed to a more integrated and efficient system. In 1899 the London, Chatham & Dover Railway (LC&D) merged with the South Eastern Railway (SED) to create the SE&C – which stood for the South Eastern & Chatham, or the 'Slow, Easy & Comfortable'.

Above: *In an age before television, popular entertainment was found at the music hall. Performances included songs, dance, novelty acts and vociferous audience participation.*

This electric revolution also made itself felt in the other spheres of public transport. The Underground system, which had begun in the 1860s with steam-drawn trains, rapidly embraced the new technology. The existing network – the Circle and District lines – converted to electricity and new electric-powered lines, tunnelled deep under the streets (rather than constructed in the old 'cut-and-cover' method), began to proliferate. The Central line between Bank and Shepherd's Bush was opened in 1900, by which time proposals for the Northern, Piccadilly and Bakerloo lines were all being advanced. The flat fare for all journeys was 2d – just under 1p.

Electric-powered vehicles also began to appear on the streets. It is important to remember that in 1900, although the world seemed poised on the brink of a new era of road transport, it was by no means clear whether this new age would be powered by electricity or by the internal combustion engine. To many, electric traction – quiet, smooth and pollution-free – seemed the more likely candidate. The horse-drawn tram system, which spread over much of outer London, began to introduce electric traction in 1900, supplying the current through

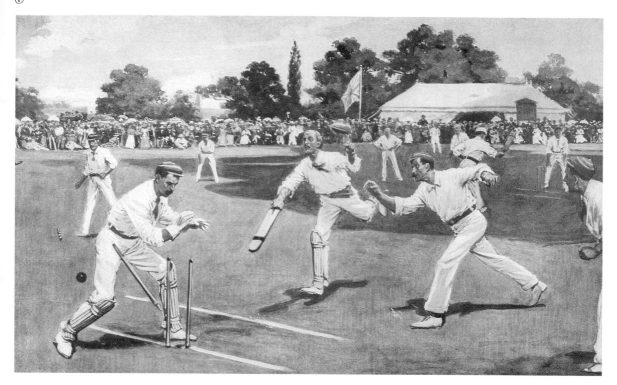

Above: *Sport was becoming an important feature of national life, and cricket was firmly established as the quintessentially British game.*

Opposite: *The motor car was still an exciting – or alarming – novelty in 1900. The first London-to-Brighton Rally was run in 1898. The recently increased speed limit of twelve miles per hour led to frequent accidents.*

overhead power-lines. And an electric cab was developed in 1897. It weighed over two tons but had a range of thirty miles between battery-recharging stops.

Motor-powered vehicles established themselves more slowly. Private cars were the preserve of wealthy enthusiasts. The first petrol-driven cabs were not developed until 1904, although, by that time, motor-omnibuses had been in operation for some seven years.

Nevertheless, despite these exciting developments, the vast majority of street traffic remained horse-drawn. The noise, the smell, the bustle of equestrian life were still pervading features of London life in 1900, features that have vanished almost entirely. Other characteristic sounds and scents of the period have vanished too: the cries of street-traders, the grinding of barrel organs, the sulphurous stench of coal-fired smogs. It is, of course, beyond the scope of a documentary to recreate such external ambience. But it is worth bringing these sensory elements to mind while considering life in the 1900 House.

Domestic life in 1900 was also changing. It was developing a new dynamic and a new direction. It was moving slowly but steadily towards the recognisably modern model. Much was still very different: most middle-class families, even those with very modest means, had at least one live-in servant. One female in ten over the age of ten was engaged in domestic service. But, in the area of family life, the picture is more recognisable. People were marrying later, and families themselves were getting smaller. In the 1850s the average family included

Motor Fiend, "WHY DON'T YOU GET OUT OF THE WAY?"
Victim, "WHAT! ARE YOU COMING BACK?"

The Village, Old Charlton.

Above: *Like many other London suburbs, Charlton preserved at its nucleus the remnants of an old rural village.*

more than five surviving children; by 1900 the number had shrunk to three. The causes of this shift are disputed: the increased knowledge of contraception, the decreased expectation of infant mortality due to improved medicine and hygiene, the increased cost of educating and supporting children – all of these probably played a part. What is clear is that this shift helped to produce a new style of family life.

Although men still tended to be the principal – if not the sole – breadwinner in most middle-class households, some of the old mid-Victorian patriarchal assumptions were being eroded. Women were coming into increased prominence both within the home and outside it. They were gaining new rights and taking on new responsibilities.

The Married Women's Property Acts of 1870 and 1882 gave them increased control of their own possessions and their own destiny, even within marriage. And other legislation continued this trend from above.

But change was also effected from within. Factors as diverse as the development of the typewriter and the expansion of the school system gave women opportunities of white-collar employment for the first time. Teachers were needed for the new high schools. And there was an ever-growing demand for stenographers in the expanding bureaucracies of metropolitan London.

The great bicycle craze of the 1890s gave women a new freedom of movement, and the chance to escape their chaperones. It also prompted a reconsideration of the restrictive dress-designs and corsetry that were then in fashion. Bloomers and divided skirts shocked conventional taste but they were easier to pedal in.

Although women were still denied the vote, the proliferation of political activity, particularly on a local level, gave them the chance of a foothold in public life. Women became active in the local commissions on public health, education and social provision. For the first time, their voices became heard on public platforms, and their abilities became recognised.

Such advances, although they pointed out a new direction, were slow and limited. It should be borne in mind that most middle-class women in 1900 still wore corsets, did not have jobs, and would have had difficulty riding a bicycle.

Nevertheless, even within the limited sphere of the house, women were forging new roles for themselves. Indeed a whole new idea of 'the home' was developed during this

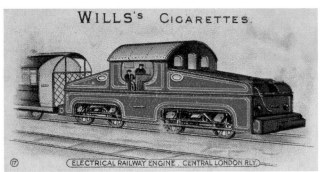

Top: *Electricity increasingly superseded gas as the means of lighting London. The powerful arc lamps illuminating the Mansion House had been in place since the 1880s.*

Above: *A 1900 cigarette card showing one of the new electric engines used on the Underground. Earlier Underground trains had been steam-powered.*

Above: *The Strand, running between London's West End and the City, was London's busiest thoroughfare.*

Below: *Bicycling became a popular activity for a whole generation of women in 1900 even though it was considered daring and 'unladylike' by some.*

period. It became less of a domestic refuge and more a stage for family life – a theatre for domestic leisure and for conspicuous consumption. And women became the stage-managers.

Their responsibilities extended from the important details of set dressing and interior decoration to the management of the daily routine and the minutiae of

cleaning. The nineteenth-century discovery of germs, microbes and bacteria, although it had opened the way for medical advance in the understanding and treatment of disease, had also created a more general alarm at the

Above: The ideal of family life was firmly established in 1900: family meals were an important part of the vision.

'invisible enemy' within the home. These twin forces worked to breed a new, and all-pervading, obsession with hygiene in many late-Victorian households. Given that the enemy was invisible (and its exact nature was not fully understood), the battle against it was never ending. Housework elaborated greatly. From the 1870s onwards there was an unending stream of household management publications, practical guides to running a house, including information on everything from napkin folding to plumbing.

Nevertheless, even among all these cares, a woman's principal role was generally conceived to be motherhood. But even here attitudes and expectations were changing. As families grew smaller, and infant mortality declined, parents – and particularly mothers – were able and willing to put more emotional investment into their children. Supported by rising incomes and the ready availability of domestic help they had, as never before, the opportunity to enjoy motherhood and to extend its bounds.

New theories about child-rearing evolved and were taken up. The old school of thought which viewed children as miniature adults needing a strict regime of rote learning, corporal

Above: *Elliscombe Road in 1900: the street was lined with trees and empty of cars, but otherwise little has changed.*

Below: *After the discovery of germs and bacteria, there was a general alarm about the 'invisible enemy' within the home.*

["Dr. MIGUEL has discovered that germs live to an advanced age."—*Weekly Paper*.]

A COUPLE OF "OLD 'UNS," SEEN THROUGH MR. PUNCH'S MICROSCOPE.

punishment, silence and respectfulness to save them from their own original sin was superseded. Childhood came to be seen as a special and privileged state, a period of charmed innocence and moral development.

The strict formality of mid-Victorian family life began to be relaxed. Children were brought more within the parental circle. Conversation was encouraged at mealtimes, rather than silence being demanded. Popular manuals on parenthood urged 'reasoning' rather than rote-learning as a means of teaching the young. Some children began addressing their parents by nicknames – or even Christian names.

A whole world of specifically childish products was developed, from children's clothes to children's books, games and toys. Play and exercise came to be seen as important parts of growing up. It is revealing that *Peter Pan*, the story of a boy who did not want to grow up, was written at this time. Childhood, compared to the standards of the past, had become pleasurable. Whether it would seem pleasurable still, when judged against the standards of the future, was for the Bowler children to discover …

A World Chronology of 1900

January

1 1900 began with a heated debate over whether 1 January represented the beginning of the last year of the nineteenth century, or the first year of the twentieth century; *The Times* placed its weight behind the former interpretation.

The Queen sent New Year's greetings to the various military commanders in South Africa, expressing her deep interest in her soldiers of all ranks. Throughout the year, coverage of the war dominated the British media.

3 The new Royal Yacht, *Victoria and Albert*, heeled over as it was being launched at Pembroke dockyard, and became jammed at the dock entrance.

4 Nigeria became a British protectorate: at Lagos, the flag of the Royal Niger Company was formally lowered, and replaced with the Union Jack.

5 The British troops in Ladysmith fought off a prolonged Boer assault.

PORTRAIT OF A CALCULATING GENTLEMAN (NOT AT ALL A BAD LOOKING CHAP) WHO HAS SOLVED THE PROBLEM AS TO WHETHER WE ARE IN THE NINETEENTH OR TWENTIETH CENTURY.

Above: Punch *was quick to satirise the debate over whether 1900 was the last year of the nineteenth century or the first year of the twentieth.*

6 The 'Gorsedd', the mystic sword of the Welsh bards, was solemnly unsheathed for the first time in over a hundred years, by the chief bard. He then invoked the blessing of God upon British arms in South Africa, and announced that the sword would remain unsheathed until the forces of righteousness had triumphed over the hordes of evil.

10 Field-Marshal Lord Roberts and his staff arrived at Cape Town. Lord Roberts replaced Sir Redvers Buller as Commander-in-Chief of the British forces in South Africa.

11 Famine raged across much of India, following poor winter rainfall: Bombay and the Central Provinces were the worst affected areas.

12 Emile Zola was presented with a gold medal (weighing four pounds) as a testimonial of his services to the cause of justice in the Dreyfus case.

The City of London Imperial Volunteers were granted the Freedom of the City, before attending a solemn service at St Paul's Cathedral and then being given supper by the Benchers of the Inner Temple. The next morning they embarked from Southampton for the Cape.

19 The Archbishop of Canterbury received a deputation from the High Church Party at Lambeth Palace. They brought a memorial, signed by 13,794 communicants of the Church of England, protesting against his adverse opinion of incense and processional lights.

20 John Ruskin, the great Victorian art-historian and moral philosopher, died at his home beside Lake Coniston, aged eighty.

24 The British, under General Warren, took Spion Kop but abandoned the position as untenable after twenty-four hours.

February

1 After ten days' fighting, a group of forts erected by rebel tribesmen in British North Borneo was stormed by a party of British and Dyaks under Captain Harington. Mat Salleh, the rebel leader, was killed and his troops taken prisoner.

8 In the City, nearly £20,000 in bank-notes was found in the pass-book of a customer at the head office of Parr's Bank. The notes formed the remainder of a sum of £60,610, which had been mysteriously 'lost' in January 1899. Of this sum £40,000 was returned anonymously a few days after the loss. Several other £100 notes had also been recovered. Now only £205 remained unaccounted for.

9 Europe was in the grip of a coal famine, caused chiefly by the great development of industry all over the continent. In London, household coal rose to 40 shillings per ton.

13 Lord Roberts crossed the River Modder, with over 50,000 men, and invaded the Orange Free State, capturing five Boer *laagers*. He continued to advance over the following days.

15 General French, with about 2000 men, reached Kimberley. The Boers hastily raised their siege, abandoning their positions, stores and ammunition, but taking their guns.

22 In the German Reichstag the Minister for War defended the practice of duelling in the army. He declared that it 'had been introduced into Germany to prevent immediate manslaughter' in case of insult. The Courts of Honour, instituted by the Emperor, had – he claimed – greatly reduced the number of duels fought.

23 In the House of Commons, a motion to censure the government for sanctioning the erection of the statue of Oliver Cromwell within the precincts of Parliament was rejected by 221 votes to fifty-three.

24 The Duke of Orleans was asked to leave England, where he was residing, after it was learnt that he had written a letter to the French caricaturist, Willette, congratulating him on some insulting pictures that he had made of Queen Victoria. His name was removed from the rolls of the London clubs to which he had been elected.

27 Colonel Cronje, one of the Boer commanders, surrendered with 4000 men to Lord Roberts.
  The Labour Representation Committee (the Labour Party) was founded.

28 Lord Dundonald with 500 mounted troops entered Ladysmith.

March

1 News of the relief of Ladysmith and the capture of Cronje's army was greeted with 'extraordinary enthusiasm' in London and throughout the country.

3 The Prince and Princess of Wales visited Shoreditch to open the final buildings of the LCC's Boundary Street scheme for housing the poor.
  The Strand and Charing Cross Electric Supply Co. works in Maiden Lane were almost completely destroyed by fire.

6 Gottlieb Daimler, the German motor-car designer and manufacturer, died.

7 The Queen gave orders that in future all ranks in the army should wear a sprig of shamrock on St Patrick's Day to commemorate the gallantry of her Irish soldiers in South Africa.

8 At the sale of the Duke of Westminster's racing stud, Flying Fox, his prize four-year-old, winner of both the Derby and the St Leger, fetched 37,500 guineas.

13 Lord Roberts entered Bloemfontein without opposition from the Boers, and was welcomed by the inhabitants.

19 Sir Arthur Evans Pritchard, the British archaeologist, began his excavations at the palace of Knossos on Crete.

20 A French force under the command of Lieutenant d'Eu attacked a strong force of Kessurians at Insala, in southern Algeria, and defeated them.

22 The Queen, accompanied by Princess Christian, travelled from Windsor to Woolwich and

Above: Ambush II, the Prince of Wales's horse, won the Grand National.

Below: The University Boat Race was an annual event that attracted the attention of all classes.

THE QUESTION OF THE HOUR.

"Wot are yer? Oxford or Cambridge?"

spent more than an hour at the Herbert Hospital, where some 700 wounded soldiers from South Africa were being treated.

24 An international chess match between Great Britain and the United States was conducted by transatlantic cable; the Americans won by six games to four.

27 The Queen received the delegates from Australia charged with overseeing the progress of the Federation Bill through the Imperial Parliament.

30 In a field of sixteen, the Grand National was won by the Prince of Wales's horse, Ambush II; it was carrying 11st 3lb.

31 The University Boat Race was won by Cambridge, who led all the way, finally defeating Oxford by twenty lengths.

Two batteries of Horse Artillery and four squadrons of the 10th Hussars and Household troops were ambushed at Koornspruit near Bloemfontein: seven guns, many stores and 250 prisoners were captured.

April

2 The 'Southern Cross' expedition into Antarctica, under M. Borchgrevink, arrived back in New Zealand, after having determined the true magnetic position of the South Pole. The sledging party reached 78 degrees 50 minutes, the furthest point south ever attained.

3 The Queen embarked on a three-week tour of Ireland, sailing on the *Victoria and Albert* to Holyhead. The following day she visited Dublin, where she was 'enthusiastically received by all classes and by the Dublin authorities'.

4 The Prince of Wales was fired at twice by a sixteen-year-old anarchist named Sipido, as he was sitting in his railway carriage at the Nord Station, Brussels. No one was hurt, the Prince remained unmoved, and the gunman was immediately arrested.

5 Colonel Bertrand occupied Igli, in the Sahara, making the French masters of Twat, and severing the area from the southern regions of Morocco.

6 In the Gold Coast, a British protectorate in West Africa, an attempt to seize 'the golden stool' of the Ashanti provoked serious disturbances throughout the region. The telegraph wires between the administrative centre, Coomassie, and the coast were cut, and the governor, Sir F. Hodgson, found himself isolated.

11 The King of the Belgians made over to the State all royal properties 'which contribute to the charms and beauty of the localities in which they are situated', on the understanding that they would be maintained as open spaces.

14 The Paris International Exhibition was opened by the President of the Republic, M. Loubet.

Above: *The Royal Yacht*, Victoria and Albert, *after it had been successfully launched.*

Below: *Southampton making a rare attack during the 1900 F.A. Cup final. They were comprehensively beaten by Bury.*

16 Violent thunderstorms passed over London and the Home Counties. At St Mary Cray, Kent, lightning struck a grandstand from which a number of people were watching a football match: one man was killed and several others injured.

20 The Ashanti and other disaffected tribes rose against British rule in the Gold Coast.

21 An attempt to blow up a lock on the Welland Canal, which connects Lakes Erie and Ontario, was thwarted. Three men were arrested. They were suspected of being American Fenians and Boer sympathisers.

In the F.A. Cup final, held at Crystal Palace, Bury beat Southampton, 4–0. Aston Villa won the First Division Championship. Woolwich Arsenal were eighth in the Second Division.

23 St George's Day was celebrated in London and elsewhere with a great display of flags on public and private buildings, and by the wearing of red and white roses.

25 A massive explosion wrecked the Boer arsenal at Johannesburg.

28 A statue of Professor T.H. Huxley was unveiled by the Prince of Wales at the Natural History Museum.

30 The British Empire League gave a banquet in honour of the Australian troops in South Africa and also for the Australian delegates visiting England. The Prince of Wales, the Duke of York and other members of the royal family attended.

   Casey Jones, the American train engineer, died.

May

7 At Naples, Mount Vesuvius erupted violently; lava flows reached the town of Torre del Greco.

9 'Presentation Day' at the University of London was held for the first time in the new Imperial College building at South Kensington. The Prince of Wales distributed the prizes.

13 The Boers besieging Mafeking attempted to carry the town by assault, but were repulsed with heavy losses.

14 Mr Chamberlain introduced the Australian Commonwealth Bill in the House of Commons: it was read for the first time.

Above: *The relief of Mafeking made Baden-Powell – or B.P. as he was affectionately known – a national hero.*

16 A madman, armed with two revolvers, a dagger and a knife, hijacked a river steamer at Stockholm. He killed seven passengers and wounded five others before escaping in a lifeboat. He was captured the following day.

17 Mafeking, after enduring seven months of siege, was relieved by Colonel Mahon; his forces inflicted a heavy defeat on the Boer besiegers.

18 News of the relief of Mafeking was greeted throughout the empire with 'intense enthusiasm'. In London, huge crowds filled the streets for the greater part of the night and the verb 'to maffick' was born.

19 Tonga was proclaimed as a British protectorate, despite the protests of the island's king.

A statue of Mr Gladstone was erected in the central hall of the Houses of Parliament; it was unveiled by Sir H. Campbell-Bannerman.

20 The Passion Play was performed for the first time at Oberammergau; over 4000 people attended.

21 The diplomatic body at Beijing called upon the Chinese government to suppress the 'Boxers', or 'The Society of Righteous and Harmonious Fists', a xenophobic military brotherhood dedicated to the expulsion of foreigners and foreign influences from China. Their atrocities against foreigners, and against Chinese converts to Christianity, had been becoming increasingly frequent in the preceding weeks.

Russia declared that it had annexed Manchuria from China.

23 The Women's Disabilities Removal Bill, enabling women to sit as councillors and aldermen on the London Borough Councils, received a second reading in the House of Commons.

24 The Queen celebrated her eighty-first birthday: there were festivities throughout the empire.

26 England and Germany agreed to build a 400-mile-long, jointly funded railway across their possessions in south-west Africa.

28 A total eclipse of the sun occurred. It could be observed most clearly in Mexico, Portugal, southern Spain and Algiers.

The Boxers, having scattered the forces sent against them, marched on Beijing.

The British annexation of the Orange Free State was formally proclaimed at Bloemfontein.

30 Johannesburg surrendered to the British after a short resistance.

The Prince of Wales's horse, Diamond Jubilee, won the Derby at Epsom.

June

4 Rodin's sculpture *The Kiss* was first exhibited publicly, in Paris.

5 Lord Roberts entered Pretoria, the capital of the Transvaal, after a day's hard fighting.

7 The Open Golf Championship, at St Andrews, was won by J.H. Taylor of Richmond. He defeated H. Vardon by 309 to 317. His last-round score of seventy-five was a new course record.

9 A force of 1500 European, American and Japanese troops landed in China and began to advance on Beijing in order to defend the foreign legations there against Boxer attacks.

13 The Boxers destroyed all foreign buildings in the eastern part of Beijing. The Custom House and the Catholic Cathedral were burnt. The foreign legations were besieged soon afterwards.

16 The Plymouth Express, travelling at over 50 miles per hour, ran into a stationary train at Slough station. Five people were killed and seventy injured.

20 Baron von Ketteler, the resident German Minister in Beijing, was murdered by the Chinese

Above: *The Plymouth Express crashes into a stationary train at Slough station.*

Below: *An Underground train carriage on the newly opened Central Line. The trains were both powered and lit by electricity.*

while on his way to negotiate for peace.

21 In America, the Republican Convention, held at Philadelphia, unanimously elected Mr McKinley as their candidate for re-election to the presidency. Colonel Theodore Roosevelt was adopted as the vice-presidential candidate.

22 The Wallace Collection of pictures, armour and works of art, in Manchester Square, London, was formally opened by the Prince and Princess of Wales.

Sir F. Hodgson, Governor of the Gold Coast, broke out of Coomassie with 600 troops and managed to reach the friendly district of Cape Coast Colony.

27 The Central Line – or Central London Electric Railway – was formally opened by the Prince of Wales. He travelled along its entire length from Bank to Shepherd's Bush; the journey took just twenty-two minutes.

29 The Lord Mayor of London hosted a lunch at the Mansion House to celebrate the completion of the *Dictionary of National Biography*, published by Messrs. Smith Elder & Co.

30 In China, the allied relief-force, under Admiral Seymour, stormed the city of Tientsin and destroyed the arsenal.

July

2 Count Zeppelin's experimental airship ascended from Friedrichshaven on Lake Constance and travelled the three and a half miles to Immarstadt.

9 A dockers' strike ended after four weeks with the unconditional surrender of the men; they waived their claim to be engaged outside the dock gates.

The Australian Federation Bill, having been passed, received the Queen's assent. The table, inkstand and pen used by Her Majesty were then presented to the representative from New South Wales to be taken back to Sydney.

15 The British garrison at Coomassie was relieved by a force under Colonel Willcocks after much fighting.

18 The Japanese volcano Mount Azuma erupted suddenly, killing over 200 people.

19 In Paris, the Metro underground railway system was opened.

23 King Alexander of Serbia announced his intended marriage to Madame Dara Maschin, a widowed lady of the court. This provoked the cabinet to resign and ex-King Milan to leave the country.

29 Five thousand Boer troops, hemmed into the Brandwater basin by Lord Roberts's forces, surrendered.

King Umberto of Italy was assassinated by an anarchist named Bresci. The king was just leaving a prize-day ceremony in the town of Monza, near Milan, when he was attacked. Bresci fired three shots from a revolver; the first struck the king in the heart.

30 In the City of London, the so-called Postman's Park, near Aldersgate, was officially opened by the Lord Mayor and the Bishop of London. Along one wall runs a 'Cloister', erected by the artist G.F. Watts, as a place where the unsung heroes of common life can be commemorated.

31 Queen Victoria's son, Prince Alfred, Duke of Edinburgh, died 'somewhat suddenly' at Rosenau Castle, Coburg.

August

2 The Shah of Persia, while on a state visit to Paris, was attacked by a would-be assassin. The man jumped on to the running board of the Shah's carriage as it was about to leave the Palais des Souverains in the Bois de Boulogne. He levelled a pistol at the Shah's breast but was disarmed – by the Grand Vizier – before he could fire.

3 Stanstead House, near Goodwood, one of the oldest mansions in Sussex, was totally destroyed by fire.

5 In China, allied forces overcame the strongly entrenched Chinese positions outside Tien-tsin.

8 The Court of Appeal, reversing an earlier judgement, decided that the Countess Cowley, who had obtained a divorce, was entitled to retain her title after her remarriage to a commoner.

10 The International Congress of Medicine and Hygiene met in Paris. Lord Lister was guest of honour.

The inaugural 'Davis Cup' – or International Lawn Tennis Trophy – was won by America.

11 In Rome, the new king, Victor Emmanuel III, took the oath of fidelity to the Constitution in the Senate Hall of the Quirinial Palace.

14 Allied forces finally relieved the foreign legations in Beijing. The Empress Dowager fled, and allied troops entered the Forbidden City.

18 Over half the workers on the Taff Vale Railway went on strike, supported by the Amalgamated Society of Railway Servants.

25 Friedrich Nietzsche, the German philosopher, died. He had been insane for the previous twelve years.

28 Two fatal cases of bubonic plague occurred in Glasgow. Ten families were removed to a reception house for observation.

29 The Taff Vale Railway dispute was provisionally settled on the understanding that all imported labour would be dispensed with inside a month.

A powerful cyclone struck Mafeking, causing more damage in ten minutes than the Boer besiegers inflicted in six months.

31 Yorkshire won the county cricket championship, having won sixteen and drawn twelve of their twenty-eight matches.

Coca-Cola was introduced to Britain.

September

1 Lord Roberts formally proclaimed the annexation of the Boer State of Transvaal to the British empire.

2 A well-attended Nationalist demonstration was held in Phoenix Park, Dublin. Resolutions were passed calling for Home Rule and the abolition of absentee landlords.

3 The Trades Union Congress was held at Huddersfield; it was attended by 388 delegates, representing 1,200,000 members.

7 In the Gold Coast, the principal Ashanti rebel chiefs surrendered unconditionally to the British relief force.

9 A hurricane devastated the coast of Texas. A tidal wave almost completely destroyed the town of Galveston. Over 4000 lives were lost on land and sea.

12 The Prince of Wales's horse, Diamond Jubilee, won the St Leger by a length and a half.

17 Eager to take advantage of popular enthusiasm for the successes in South Africa, Lord Salisbury called a general election.

19 The Manchester Central Post Office was destroyed by fire when the building's electric wires fused.

21 The Commissioners for Her Majesty's Woods and Forests bought the ruins of Tintern Abbey, together with over 2000 acres of surrounding land, from the Duke of Beaufort. The whole site was to be preserved for the enjoyment of the public.

22 The Socialist Congress met in Paris; it was attended by a large body of delegates from many countries.

October

Above: *The beginnings of the heritage industry: the ruins of Tintern Abbey.*

2 The International Peace Conference, assembled at Paris, passed a resolution declaring that the responsibility for the war in South Africa fell upon Great Britain for repeatedly refusing arbitration.

8 Lord Ranfurley, Governor of New Zealand, landed at Raratonga, and – at the unanimous request of the chiefs and people – formally annexed the Cook Islands.

11 Count Henri de la Vaulx won the French ballooning competition. Starting from Vincennes in northern France he reached Koroslycheff, near Kiev, in thirty-six hours.

13 In Russia the Tsar received special envoys from the Dalai Lama of Tibet.

16 The so-called Khaki Election was completed: the Conservatives won 362 seats, the Liberal Unionists sixty-nine, the Liberals 187, and the Nationalists eighty-two. The result marked a net gain of two seats for the Conservative alliance. The MP for Greenwich (and hence 50 Elliscombe Road), Colonel Lord Hugh Cecil (Con.), was returned with an increased majority.

25 A memorial window to Geoffrey Chaucer was unveiled at St Saviour's Church, Southwark, on the 500th anniversary of the poet's death.

29 The City Imperial Volunteers landed at Southampton and were brought to Paddington. They then marched through cheering crowds to St Paul's Cathedral for a thanksgiving service. There followed a reception at the Guildhall and then a banquet at the premises of the Royal Artillery Company. Due to the crowding in the streets there were over 1000 casualties, two of them fatal.

November

1 Municipal elections took place for the first time in the new London boroughs created under the recent Act. In the twenty-eight boroughs: 785 Conservatives (or Moderates); 460 Liberals (or Progressives); 160 Independents, and eleven Labour members were elected. Charlton, one of eight wards in Greenwich, returned one Progressive and six Moderate councillors.

6 In America, the Republican, President McKinley, was re-elected.

9 At the Lord Mayor's banquet Lord Salisbury, the Prime Minister, urged the need for 'constant watchfulness abroad and preparedness at home.'

An election was held to choose the mayors for the twenty-eight new Metropolitan Borough Councils. Fourteen Conservatives, eight Liberals and six Independents were chosen.

13 The Ogaden Somalis, in British East Africa, rose up against the British government, and a force of about 4000 attacked the British sub-commissioner at Kismayer.

14 The French Senate confirmed a new law admitting the right of women to practise at the French bar.

16 As the German Emperor was driving through the streets of Breslau, a madwoman threw an axe at him; it struck the carriage.

At Johannesburg, five Italians, four Greeks and one Frenchman were arrested and charged with conspiring to plant a bomb in St Mary's Church during a service which Lord Roberts was expected to attend.

22 Arthur Sullivan, the composer who collaborated with W.S. Gilbert on a succession of popular operas, died.

29 The triennial elections of the London School Board were held. Twenty-eight Progressives were returned, twenty-five Moderates and two Roman Catholics.

30 Lord Roberts formally handed over the command of South Africa to Lord Kitchener. Oscar Wilde died in Paris.

December

3 The new session of Parliament was opened.

5 The German Emperor issued an edict substituting English for French as a compulsory subject in Prussian secondary schools.

13 Boer forces drove General Clements and his troops back from Magliesberg, near Pretoria.

31 The century closed with a terrible gale. One of the upright stones supporting a lintel of the outer circle of Stonehenge fell. The last time such an incident occurred was in 1759.

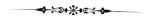

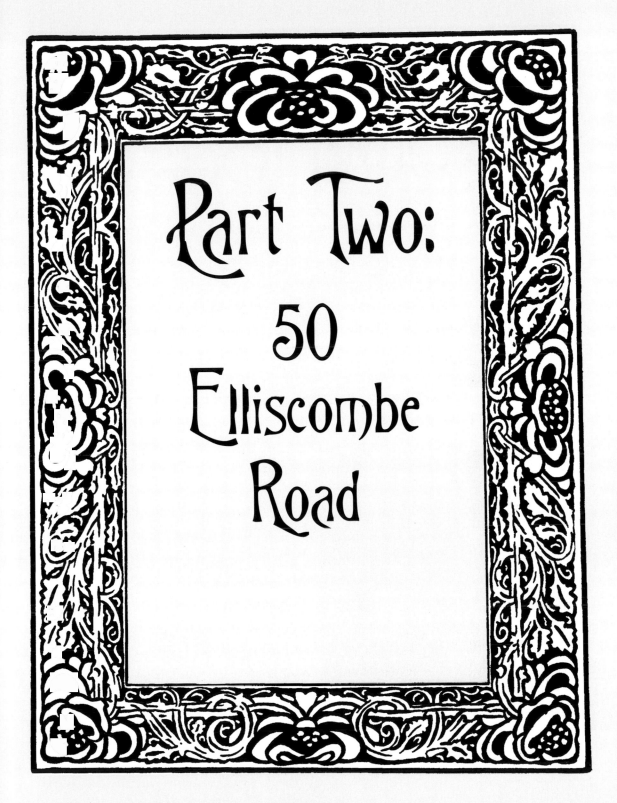

Part Two:

50 Elliscombe Road

Restoring the 1900 House

❦⟶⟨※⟩⟵❦

House restoration – like football – is a team game. And the team assembled for the 1900 House project was an impressive one. It needed to be. The challenge of creating a fully furnished turn-of-the-century house, accurate in every detail, from the paint finishes and lighting systems to the table linen and toothbrushes, was enormous. It called for different disciplines, different areas of expertise, and a great deal of hard work.

Overseeing the architectural side of the restoration was Peter Riddington, of Donald Insall Associates. He had been responsible for restoring five of the State Rooms at Windsor Castle, following their devastation by fire. His expertise and attention to detail in recreating the splendours of that Grade I scheduled monument were now to be directed towards a rather more modest domestic space. On the practical front were the builders, Holloway White Allom, who were charged with making the vision real.

The detailed historical information on every aspect of 1900 domestic life and décor was provided by the historian Daru Rooke, Director of the Armley Mills Museum in Leeds. And the daunting task of finding all the items required – from the enamelled bathtub to the authentic coffee grinder – was assigned to Lia Kramer, an experienced art director for film and television.

Above: *Lia Kramer, the art director, who found all the furnishings for the house, putting the finishing touches to the décor.*

Around these core members stood a ring of other experts, whose knowledge could be called on to elucidate such specialist areas as food, costume, medicine and the garden.

The first task, however, was very broad indeed: it was necessary to find a suitable house – modest, suburban and built in the last decade of the nineteenth century. Charlton, the south-east London suburb, was decided upon as an appropriate location. The whole area had been developed at the right time; it still maintained much of its original look and, indeed, its original character. The local high street could still boast a local butcher, a local greengrocer, a local baker. And, as a historical reference point, it was located not far from Greenwich, the site of the controversial Millennium Dome.

Nevertheless, having chosen the location, it took some time to find the house. The team looked at dozens. Some were too large, others too odd, or too 'mucked about'. Number 50 Elliscombe Road was different.

Top: *Peter Riddington, the architect, a specialist in restoring old buildings.*

Above: *George Cox, the builder, brought professional expertise – and personal knowledge – to the job.*

'We knew at once that it was just right,' recalled Peter. An unpretentious two-storey red-brick terraced house with a bay window at the front and a little garden at the back, it was completely characteristic of the speculative developments at the time. The majority of houses in London would have looked like that in 1900. It is not too much to say that they still do a hundred years on.

The house, along with the rest of the street, had been built in the mid 1890s by a single builder–developer. It had been intended as a family home for one of the great – and growing – army of white-collar workers needed in London at the time. Later the single dwelling had been divided into two flats, one on the ground floor, the other on the first. The staircase had been boarded in, and two inner 'front doors' erected side by side inside the hall, one leading up the stairs, the other leading further on down the hallway.

With two flats in the building, facilities had to be duplicated. A kitchen was put in on the first floor, and a WC was plumbed into the bathroom. Downstairs a brick extension was added to the back of the house to provide another bathroom.

Following the conversion little further work had been carried out on the property. The upper flat had been almost untouched except by paint. The downstairs flat was refurbished in the late 1970s or early 80s (judging on stylistic grounds). The panelled doors were covered over with flush hardboard, while the ceiling was stuck with polystyrene tiles – in the mistaken belief, Peter suggested, that this would reduce any noise from above. In fact it would serve only to make the room itself quiet and, thus, any noise from the flat above more intrusive.

Opposite: *Before work began: the basic fabric was all intact, but the garden wall and the white woodwork would have to go.*

Upstairs it was clear that many original features still survived: door furniture, fireplaces, mouldings, the etched glass in the bathroom. Downstairs the picture was less clear.

The first task was to strip out all the obviously modern accretions. The back addition had to be taken down. 'When we told the council what we intended to do,' recalled Peter, 'they said that they had no knowledge of any back addition at Number 50. It had obviously been knocked up without planning permission.' The relatively poor quality of the job was also revealed by the fact that the only rot in the whole building was found in the back-addition door. The original fabric of the house was all in good condition.

Inside the house the restorative work was equally dramatic: fireplaces were opened up and ceilings taken down; hardboard coverings were prised away. The partition wall between the two flats was removed, and the staircase was once more made open to the hallway.

The central heating system and all the radiators were taken out; so, too, were all the electrical switches, sockets and fittings. The electrical removal had, however, to be only a cosmetic operation. The system itself had to remain, along with a few discreet power points, in order to power the concealed cameras that would be necessary to record the doings of the Bowler family in their 1900 home.

As demolition work progressed, tantalising clues began to emerge of how the house used to be: original fireplaces lurked behind unpromising hardboard screens; old decorative schemes were discovered hidden behind layers of paper and paint. An example of the hallway's original wallpaper was found inside the linen cupboard on the first floor. 'We didn't want to get too bogged down in recreating exactly what had existed at 50 Elliscombe Road in 1900,' explained

Daru. 'Our aim was to create a generic house – a sort of Barratt home of the period.' Nevertheless the archaeological information revealed during the building – or un-building – work was very useful.

The team was also able to fill in some of the gaps in its knowledge by visiting other houses in the street. Elliscombe Road was all developed at the same time, and although the developer seems to have introduced a few minor variations, the basic arrangement and design of the neighbouring houses is the same. Some had been more fortunate than others in retaining their original features. 'We went on a tour of the neighbourhood,' recalled Peter. 'People were very helpful. We found out a great deal. There were homes that had kept their outside lavatories, others that still had built-in kitchen dressers, or stained-glass features in the doors.'

In tandem with these discoveries about the layout and décor of the house, Daru was piecing together information from contemporary sources. Literary works such as *The Diary of a Nobody* and *The History of Mr Polly* offered some telling glimpses of how houses were lived in, but they tended to take too much knowledge for granted. More richly rewarding were the great domestic encyclopaedias that were such a feature of the period. These enormous tomes give practical information on every aspect of house decoration and home life: how to stock a linen cupboard or greet a bishop; what to cover the hall stairs with and when to grow a beard.

This sort of information was vital. It was necessary for Daru to build up a picture of a 1900 house from the inside, to understand the way in which rooms were used, and the concerns of the people who would have used them, rather than merely gathering together an accumulation of period objects. For the late Victorians decoration and design tended to be directed

Opposite: *At the back of the house an ugly extension had been 'knocked up' to provide a downstairs bathroom.*

by function. It would have been possible to dress up a room so that, superficially, it looked very 1900, but it was only by understanding the underlying motives of the original inhabitants that a truly authentic scheme could be evolved.

Cassell's *Book of the Household*, a four-volume part-work first brought out in the 1890s, became a bible for Daru and the rest of the team. From it they were able to build up – room by room – a picture of the dominating concerns of 1900 home life. And it also provided them with all the appropriate details of décor and furnishing, enabling them to draw up lists of the objects required to fit out a 1900 kitchen or dress up a 1900 parlour.

There was recognition, too, of the historical process involved in the decorations. At a time when the vast majority of people rented their homes, the main decorative scheme would have been put in by the landlord, who was often also the developer. It would reflect his taste, his sense of economy, his desire to make an impressive show with the minimum expense. This base would then be overlaid by the furnishings and flourishes of the family living in the house. They would be eager to exert their own style, but reluctant to engage in major – or permanent – schemes of decoration.

The lists of objects put together by Daru were, as Lia recalled, 'endless'. And finding everything on them was an incredible undertaking. No source could be left untapped. For the larger items – baths, fireplaces, kitchen fixtures – Lia used a network of salvage merchants. She also developed a constant vigilance. As she soon came to realise, 1900 is not that long ago. A lot of stuff still remains *in situ*. Most people have something from 1900 in their home.

Above: *Although they had not been used for over sixty years, the original gas fittings were still in place on the walls.*

Sometimes old objects find new uses. Old mangles and coppers and baths often end up as 'features' in people's gardens.

Companies that specialise in hiring out period objects and furniture for film productions were a potentially rich resource. Lia, however, was concerned not to rely too heavily on them: 'I wanted the family to feel that the stuff in the house was theirs – that they could break it without having to worry.' Instead, she devoted herself to scouring antique shops and early-morning flea markets in search of appropriate items. The search itself was like a roller-coaster, she recalled. The list kept on getting longer and longer, the objects more and more obscure. 'There was almost a "challenge" element to it,' recalled Lia. For specialised items – such as pens or clocks or games – Lia relied on experts for advice and assistance. As she discovered, however, specialists always tend to like the exceptional and the rare. They would sometimes be disappointed that she was after the typical and the common.

The challenge of the search was made more intense by the various restraints imposed by the project. The budget was limited. Everything had to be done for £35,000 (all the furniture was later sold to help with the costs). It might seem a lot at first glance, but it is really quite a modest sum with which to furnish and dress a whole house with antique fittings. This, of course, was in line with the illusion that the house had been fitted out by a canny developer and an unpretentious middle-class family on a limited budget. But some discrepancies did creep into the equation.

Prices and values have shifted over the century. Items that were comparatively cheap in 1900 have become very expensive to buy or to replicate. Colour-printed wallpapers that were a penny a roll a hundred years ago are now close to a hundred pounds a roll. The process does, of course, work the other way around too. Old kitchen utensils are, comparatively, cheaper than they were.

The team was very conscious that the house must be safe for the Bowler family to live in, while recognising that many aspects of 1900 living required rather more care and vigilance than is generally exercised in a modern home. A limit had to be set on the authenticity of some materials. Lead-based paint was thought to be too dangerous to use on the wall surfaces, although it would have been there in 1900. And, when it was decided to re-install gas lighting throughout the ground floor, the fittings needed close attention. The builders were very excited to discover all the original gas-piping still buried in the plasterwork of the walls but, although this was very useful in showing where the gas-fittings had originally been sited, not all the actual piping could be re-used. The standard gas pressure had changed since 1900, when we moved from town to natural gas. The pipes need to be of a different gauge to carry it safely.

As a further precaution various concealed alarm devices were installed: a gas detector, a carbon-monoxide detector, a fire detector (not to mention a conventional intruder alarm). The plan for a smoke alarm, however, had to be dismissed on the ground floor; what with the coal fires, candles, oil lamps and cooking range it would have been going off continually.

Despite this close concern for the safety aspects of the work, a visit from the local Health and Safety inspector served as a stark reminder of just how protected we now are by regulations and recommendations compared to our forebears. If the inspector had had his way there would have been no gas lighting, no oil lamps, no coal-fired range. He disapproved of the rugs on the shiny floor surfaces, and had grave doubts about the wisdom of stocking the bathroom cupboard with a cut-throat razor.

Nevertheless he was gradually won over on these points, as he came to understand

Above: *The coal-hole cover just by the front step; plans to use it had to be abandoned because of safety concerns about access to the cellar via a narrow flight of stairs.*

the nature of the project and the conscientiousness with which both the design team and the Bowler family were approaching it. One major sticking point, however, was the coal cellar. It had been hoped to use this for storing the family coal supply. The coal could even have been delivered into it, direct, through the coal hole in front of the house. But access to the cellar was via a very steep flight of narrow steps leading down from under the hall stairs; and the cellar itself was pitch black. It was thought, by the Health and Safety inspector, to be too much to expect someone (perhaps wearing a long skirt) to get up and down these stairs while holding a coal scuttle and a lamp – even though the 1900 inhabitants would have managed it. Reluctantly the team bowed to this pressure: two coal bunkers were constructed in the back garden.

Such unforeseen additions put increased pressure on an already tight schedule. Time was pressing. The whole task of refurbishment had to be carried out in barely three months. Everything had to be done at once. Lia was searching for fittings that the builders were waiting to install. 'It was a real dash to get everything ready on time,' she recalled. Last-minute crises with the hall wallpaper and the fireplace in the front room created added drama. 'It got a bit chaotic at times,' Daru admitted. 'Major building work would be happening at the same time as we were trying to finish off the smallest details.' To make matters more complex the camera crew were trying to record the scene, and inevitably that slowed things down even more.

The work, however, was finished on time: the last drawer of the kitchen dresser was filled, the framed photographs were arranged on the mantelpiece, the sheet music was put on the piano. The illusion was complete. The stage was set and the drama itself was ready to begin.

Above: *The diamond-patterned tiles and beaded edging on the front path were still in good condition when the house was found.*

Below: *The front door at 50 Elliscombe Road was one of several in the street to retain its panels of simple, but characteristic, stained glass.*

Above: *The original gilded numbering, though slightly worn, was still clearly visible in the glass light over the front door.*

The façade

Externally, the front of the house needed very little work to bring it back to how it would have been in 1900. The concrete roof tiles, it is true, were something of an anachronism – ideally Peter would have liked to change them back to slate. Some of the other houses in the street still had their original slates and looked the better for it. But the limits of budget and time put such major work out of reach.

More easily addressed was the woodwork. The prevailing contemporary habit of painting all external woodwork white was largely unknown in 1900. Colour tended to be used much more boldly then. So, for the wooden surrounds and other timber detailing Daru selected a rich colour scheme of maroon with cream edging, using paints developed by Dulux for their Heritage range.

The front door, however, was not included in this scheme. Close inspection of the paint layers on the door suggested that it had been 'wood-grained' – painted with an elaborate finish in two tones of brown to create the illusion of rich hardwood. One of Holloway White Allom's skilled painter-decorators, Hughie, was able to reproduce the effect. This use of illusion – of cheap materials suggesting more expensive ones – was a recurrent theme of late-Victorian décor. It reappeared in a variety of forms throughout the house.

The original gilded lettering for the number '50' in the light above the door was faded but still visible. It was readily repainted. The original chequered black and terracotta tiles leading up to the front door were also still in place.

'We tend to assume that Victorian front gardens had low walls and railings,' explained Peter, 'but this is only because low walls and railings tend to survive.' Having discovered some old photographs of Elliscombe Road, the team was intrigued to discover that many of the houses were originally fronted with very simple, high wooden fences. Nearly all of these have vanished. Nevertheless – working from the photos – it was possible to recreate the original design and to stain it with a preservative coat of creosote.

The hallway

Major alterations were needed to return the hallway to its original form. The whole space had been hacked about when the house had been divided into flats. The partition wall and the two flat doors had to be removed. The partition had run up the side of the staircase and it was hoped that the original banister might have been preserved within the thickness of the wall. Sadly it was not. There were, however, traces left to show how it had been constructed and, indeed, painted.

In many middle-class homes the newel post and the handrail would have been made from hardwood while the other rails of the banister would have been made from softwood, grained to look like hardwood. The Elliscombe Road development, however, was one step down from this level. There was enough evidence remaining to show that the newel post was in wood-grained softwood, and that the other rails were merely softwood painted dark brown. It was easy enough to recreate this effect.

Above: *The front hall had been partitioned to provide separate access to the upstairs and ground-floor flats.*

Above right: *Once the partitioning had been stripped out, the original layout of the hall became clearer. Unfortunately the bannisters had been removed.*

More difficult to replicate were the missing 'console brackets' which should have been supporting the short beam running across the hall ceiling above the foot of the stairs. Also obliterated was the simple 'rope' moulding on the plasterwork of the beam itself. Neighbouring houses, however, had preserved both these features intact. The builders were able to take impressions of the brackets and moulding from the hallway of the house next door. From these they could make their own moulds and recast the pieces of plasterwork.

The general decorative scheme of the hallway would have been the work of the developer. It was directed by the twin concerns of the period: show and hygiene. Linoleum was used on the floor and a varnished wallpaper was chosen for the walls. Both would have been favoured by a 1900 house-dweller as being easy to wipe clean. The lino, however, was patterned to

look like the parquet that might be found in the hallway of a superior dwelling. Similarly all the doors leading off the hallway were grained to look more impressive.

Above: *The beam above the foot of the stairs was missing some of its decorative details.*

Old paint layers showed that the stair treads had originally been painted with a rather crude fake marble effect. But the team thought that it might be taking matters too far to recreate this. Instead they opted for a plain, dark paint finish, either side of a stair carpet.

For decorative purposes the team followed the late-Victorian convention of dividing the walls in the hallway into three bands, with a dado rail and picture rail. Neither the division nor the rails remained in the hallway, but traces of the dado arrangement survived in the linen cupboard on the first floor, and the picture rail was still in place in the upstairs bedroom. Following these clues, they were able to recreate the scheme almost exactly.

Below the dado rail a dark brown textured paper ran down to the dark brown skirting board. A floral-patterned varnished paper was hung in the broad area between the dado and the picture rail. And then the space above the picture rail was painted white, making it merge into the white painted ceiling.

Finding a suitable floral-patterned wallpaper for the space between dado and picture rail proved to be one of the major headaches of the whole conversion. And yet matters began so well. A trace of the original paper – a gold and brown floral pattern – was discovered inside the cupboard on the landing. This was something of a coup. There was a hope that an exact match could be found. Period wallpapers are still reproduced – indeed, several of the established wallpaper companies have been in business since the 1890s and have kept some of their designs in almost continuous production.

Lia soon discovered, however, that it tends to be the top-of-the-range designs that are still reproduced. Cheaper papers – which were often quite bold and garish – are thought to be less acceptable to modern taste. The original hall wallpaper was anything but top-of-the-range; it was not still in production. Nevertheless Lia was able to trace a very satisfactory substitute

Above: *The built-in cupboard at the top of the stairs was an unexpected treasure-trove of information: it contained traces of the original wallpaper.*

from a company specialising in period paper designs. There matters rested – and rested. Lia began to be concerned when the paper that she had ordered had not turned up after two months. She rang to chase the order only to discover that the wallpaper factory had burnt down, and no one had told her.

After a frantic search, an alternative supplier was found. But then they failed to meet their delivery date. Disaster loomed. The job was supposed to have been completed. Only at the eleventh hour, after much pleading and bullying, did the paper finally arrive. It was speedily hung, just in time to dazzle the Bowlers as they came through the front door.

An only slightly less stressful element of the décor was the lighting. Lia was delighted to discover a little four-sided stained-glass gaslight lampshade. 'It was just the sort of thing that any modest middle-class family would have had in their hall.' With that characteristic mixture of show and economy, the stained-glass motif was fixed only on one side: the side facing out towards the front door and the street. The other three sides were plain. Although such shades would once have been both common and cheap, they are now sought-after items. Lia was shocked, though not completely surprised, to discover that the dealer wanted over £500 for it. Such a price would have unbalanced the budget, so Lia was obliged to bend her own guidelines and hire a similar light shade from a film hire repository.

Among other items of hall furniture Lia was asked to find a hat-and-umbrella stand. The one she discovered is an imposing wooden-backed model that stands flush to the wall. It has plenty of room for the heavy overcoats and bulky umbrellas that were the norm in an age before synthetic fabrics.

The kitchen

Refurbishing the kitchen was the team's biggest task. Of all rooms the kitchen has perhaps changed most in the past hundred years, both in the way it looks and the way in which it is used.

At Elliscombe Road the original kitchen space had been converted into a dining-cum-

breakfast room, while what had been the 'scullery' area beyond it was used as the kitchen proper. As a result it was fairly easy to clear the kitchen space prior to restoration. There were no major services to be removed, and the only built-in fixture – a narrow cupboard to the right of the chimney breast – turned out to be an original feature. The ceiling plaster did, however, have to be replaced. It was in poor condition largely because the bathroom was overhead; inevitable spillages over the years had taken their toll.

Having cleared the space, two major fittings then had to be installed – the key items in any 1900 kitchen: a coal-fired range and a built-in dresser. The chimney breast, where the range would have stood, had been boarded up, probably in the 1930s, and a gas-fire mounted on the front of it. The fire was removed and the space reopened, ready to receive a new range.

Top: *Little remained of the original kitchen, except for the narrow built-in cupboard to the right of the chimney-breast.*

Above: *The chimney-breast, which had been filled in and boarded up, needed to be reopened to receive the range.*

Above: *The hub of any late-Victorian household: the coal-fired range. It cooked the food, heated the water, and kept the kitchen warm.*

It had to wait some time. The search for a suitable model proved long and tortuous. The specifications were exacting: it had to be in working order, of the right period and the right style; it needed to be a model with a back-boiler so that it could heat water for both the kitchen and the upstairs bathroom, and it needed to fit within the chimney breast.

Lia began her search in optimistic mood. 'Initially I thought it was going to be quite easy,' she recalled. 'But it turned into a real quest.' Lots of ranges were available but none could meet all her criteria. Lia gathered whole books of photos of ranges from a wide network of salvage men and antique dealers, without discovering one that would work for Elliscombe Road. 'I saw so many different models that I became a complete "anorak" about ranges,' she admitted. There were quite a lot of ranges available in the north of England, where people seemed to have held on to them for longer, because coal was so plentiful and cheap up there. But they

were of a different type to London ranges; they had open rather than closed fireboxes.

Above: *Lia and Daru inspect the range, to check that it is in full working order, ready for the Bowlers' arrival…*

Lia also found disconcerting the fact that there were such wide fluctuations in the prices she was quoted. She came to the conclusion that there is not really a market price for an old range. She was quoted from £250 to £1800 for pieces that were very similar. Lia also developed her own theory about some of the higher prices. 'Some people, I think, latched on to my southern accent and to the mention of a television series and put prices up a bit.'

Eventually, after numerous false hopes, Lia did find a range in an antique shop in Northampton; it was the right date and – crucially – the right size. It was in quite good condition, but it had really been preserved as a decorative feature rather than as a working piece. It needed to be restored for use. A back-boiler had to be specially built and attached.

Perhaps inevitably, three days after buying the Northamptonshire range and setting in train its restoration, Lia saw another suitable model, in even better condition, outside a junk shop in London's Holloway Road, just around the corner from where she lives!

If finding the range was problematic, so too was installing it. The back-boiler had to be connected not only to a tap at the side of the range, but also to the bathroom upstairs. Because this water-heating system was to be 'gravity-fed' rather than operated by pump, the pipes carrying the water between the range and the bathroom needed to be much larger than is usual nowadays. Burying these 2½-inch tubes in the wall plaster was a messy and time-consuming business.

Installing the dresser was rather less problematic. From their visits to neighbouring houses where original dressers were still in place, Peter and the rest of the team knew exactly how

Above: *The kitchen dresser provided storage for table linen and dishes, a showcase for china and a narrow work surface.*

the dresser should look (simple, wooden and gloss-painted) and where it should go (in the alcove to the left of the chimney breast). A rough design was drawn up: cupboards below (for pots), a row of drawers (for table linen), a counter (for the breadboard) and shelves (for displaying crockery). Then a carpenter brought the wood in and constructed the dresser on site, after which it was painted – like all the other woodwork in the kitchen – with a dark brown oil-based paint.

Next to the dresser was a fitted cupboard which had been the larder or pantry. The hardboard cladding which covered its outside edge was stripped off to reveal the original grooved panelling underneath, as well as two rows of ventilation holes. In the absence of a fridge, the larder would help the Bowlers to preserve food. A special marble shelf, on which bowls of cold water could be placed, offered a further cooling device.

The narrow cupboard to the right of the range was also stripped of its hardboard coverings and painted; the two upper cupboard doors were discovered to have been glazed, and were duly restored to that condition.

The kitchen surfaces – walls, floor and ceiling – all needed special attention to give them a distinctive 1900 aspect. Hygiene was the prime concern: everything had to be smooth and washable. Varnished paper was again used for the walls. In an attempt to suggest a rather higher grade of wall covering it was printed to look like light oak panelling. A similar deception was effected with the linoleum on the floor – it was printed with a chequered tile motif. As in the hallway the lino was quite crudely 'whacked down' on top of the existing floorboards.

A rag rug was found to go in front of the range. This was a common feature in kitchens. The absorbent quality of the rug soaked up any minor slops or spillages, and prevented the floor from becoming slippery.

The ceiling was painted with plain white distemper. This traditional method of using chalk or pigment, bound in egg-white-based wash, was used on ceilings throughout the house, as it certainly would have been in 1900. As a paint finish it has several advantages. It is cheap, easy to apply and it does not absorb damp.

Work surfaces were at a premium in a late-Victorian kitchen. The main shelf of the dresser was generally used only for slicing the bread (which was kept on it). Most actual work was done on the kitchen table. Lia found a good example with sturdy legs and a thick top.

Above: *This useful domestic aide-memoire was one of Lia's best finds. The items listed bring the 1900 world vividly to life.*

Stocking the kitchen was an exacting – and ever-expanding – job. Lia had to gauge what, in practical terms, the family would need: how many plates, spoons, saucepans and teacups. Then she had to discover authentic 1900 examples of these objects, and in a condition that would allow them to be used.

She was frequently challenged – and surprised. 'I found an old list at the Victoria and Albert Museum Library describing how to fit out a kitchen. It seemed enormous. But when I went back home and checked it off against my own kitchen, I found that I had *exactly* the same number of saucepans, plates and utensils as they suggested. After that I just kept thinking how I lived and worked in my kitchen and then working out from that what the Bowlers might need. It all worked quite well, except that I left out the soup bowls; I'm not a great soup eater myself.'

Research revealed that enamel saucepans were as widely used in the 1890s and 1900s as they were in later decades. The colours, however, were always changing. Each decade seems to have developed its own distinctive colour-code, based on variations of pale blue, white, brown and black. The prevailing colour-way around 1900 was black exteriors and grey interiors. This

Above: *The restored kitchen with the scullery beyond. The range would have made it a hot place to work during the summer months The rag rug is typical of a Victorian kitchen.*

narrowed Lia's options considerably. 'I had to turn down black pans with white interiors, and blue pans with grey interiors; they would have been the wrong period.'

Putting together a collection of 1900 table-linen brought Lia into an unexpectedly intimate proximity with the past. Tablecloths and napkins were often beautifully hand-stitched and embroidered. 'There was so much love and care in these small items,' she recalled. 'And there was me buying them at a flea market for next to nothing. It sometimes made me a bit sad.'

The list of things to find sometimes seemed never-ending. Daru was forever suggesting new items to search for: coffee grinders, egg whisks, weighing scales. A whole armoury of brushes had to be found for all the different and specific cleaning tasks demanded by a 1900 kitchen.

Lia was particularly pleased to discover a specially constructed 'shopping list memorandum board' of almost exactly the right period, complete with such now unfamiliar staples as loaf sugar, potted meat, grate polish and dentifrice.

Some compromises did have to be made. Health considerations meant that they stocked the kitchen with stainless steel kitchen knives rather than authentic steel ones which would have been liable to rust even with constant care. And a few things escaped the net altogether. 'I never did find an appropriate tea strainer,' Lia admits.

The scullery

The sink in a late-Victorian house would not have been in the kitchen but in an adjoining scullery. The room would also have served as a laundry for wash days. The scullery space at Elliscombe Road had been converted into the kitchen of the downstairs flat. It was crowded with the usual modern kitchen conveniences – built-in cupboards, a cooker and fridge. These had to be removed.

The original back door, leading out into the garden, had been taken out when the back-addition had been built. It needed to be restored. An old-fashioned, semi-glazed door, similar in design to the ones surviving at the back of other houses in the street, was installed. The glass in the panels was stronger than it would have been a hundred years ago to comply with modern safety standards.

Finding an old square-sided ceramic sink was easy enough. There are still many around. And even if some

Below: *What had been the scullery was being used as a small, cramped kitchen for the downstairs flat.*

Above: *The built-in washing copper involved much work to research, design and build, and even more to use.*

of them have been converted into flower tubs they can be readily converted back again. The real challenge was the copper, a large built-in washing cauldron set above its own fire. The house would definitely have had one, but there was no available evidence to suggest what it would have looked like. Some of the neighbouring houses preserved traces to suggest where the copper would have stood in the scullery, but there were no intact examples surviving.

The whole thing had to be built up piece by piece. Lia found an actual copper cauldron early on in the proceedings. Daru studied old pictures of operating coppers and worked out a basic design for setting the cauldron above a built-in furnace. Peter then drew this up as a more formal plan, which the builder – George Cox – then worked from, supplementing it with his own memories of coppers seen in his childhood.

The result certainly looked great, but it also had to work, and work safely. It was clear from some of the vestigial remains at other houses in the street that the flue from the original copper would have run up into the chimney of the upstairs back bedroom. But this arrangement would not be allowed now for health and safety reasons. Instead, a separate iron flue had to be run from the furnace up the outside of the building. The undertaking – from design to completion – was one of the major pieces of work carried out at the house. The copper at Elliscombe Road must be the first one built in London for many, many years.

The walls of the scullery were painted in a wonderful pale-blue distemper, a traditional colour for laundries as it made whites look even whiter. The floor was covered with simple terracotta tiles which could survive having water slopped on to them.

As an aid to any washing that might be done, Lia found several bizarre-looking plungers or 'dolly paddles', as well as a hefty mangle. There are still quantities of mangles about; they are so big and heavy that they are hard to get rid of. Some have made new lives for themselves as garden features – but an outdoor life does nothing to improve their working mechanisms. Lia found her one neglected at the back of someone's garage.

The water closet

In 1900 a WC in the back garden would have been an important selling feature for the house. London was very proud of the sewerage system that it had developed in the second half of the nineteenth century. Earth closets had been largely superseded by flush lavatories, certainly in all new developments. Nevertheless these WCs continued to be sited outside the house proper, in the back garden, because Victorians were suspicious of the illnesses that could be caused by an inside toilet.

Although at Number 50 the WC had been re-established in the bathroom at some time in the 1930s and the brick privy in the garden demolished, many of the other houses in the street still retained their old outhouses. Thus it was possible for the team to recreate something almost identical to what would have been there originally.

The salvage yards yielded up a spectacular old 'vitreous china' bowl and cistern; the walls were painted with the same blue distemper used in the scullery, and the door with the same maroon oil-based paint used on all

Above: *The brick 'privy' was set up in the garden using the foundations of the demolished extension.*

the other external woodwork. There was no provision for lighting or heating. But at least the wooden seat would have slightly reduced the chill factor on cold mornings.

The back garden

To transform the wilderness at the back of the house into an authentic 1900 garden, the team called on the services of Katy Butler, the head gardener at Yalding Organic Gardens and an expert on garden history. The brief was a difficult one, constrained not least by the limits of time and space. The whole transformation had to be effected in under two months, and the plants chosen needed to be at their best during the period of filming – between March and May. But before anything could begin the whole area had to be dug over and enriched with 'a great deal of cow muck'.

Although most of the garden was empty, the space was encumbered by a large bank at the far end, and by a paved pathway running along the right-hand side. Both were too big to move in the time available so Katy decided to hide the bank and adapt the path.

Working out an authentic period design also posed special problems, not least because most of the available information on 1900 gardens concerned large and important establishments. Katy did, however, discover a useful source in Cassell's *Popular Gardening*, a best-selling book dating from the turn of the century. From this she began to build up a picture of the sort of

Above: *A formal back garden gradually began to take shape in the wilderness behind the house.*

garden a 1900 suburban family would have aspired to. Contrary to expectations she discovered that typical suburban families of the time – rather than making informal cottage-style gardens – strove to imitate, on a small scale, the formal effects of grander gardens. Gardens were places for show and relaxation. They were meant to look impressive, not least from the windows of the house.

Most middle-class families were relieved from the necessity of growing their own food, but some still liked to maintain a small vegetable patch. Katy was able to incorporate this feature into her design by dividing the long garden-space into a series of compartments, separated by trellised screens.

In the area nearest the house she laid out a small, formal lawn with a diamond-shaped flowerbed in the centre. She set a standard rose at the centre of this, and then planted winter-bedding plants around it, including pansies, cerastium and bellis. The colour scheme for this was red, white and blue – an apt reflection of late-Victorian patriotism. Beside the now-gravelled pathway she planted a scented border dominated by a row of sweet peas. She was pleased to discover that these echoed the pattern of the wallpaper chosen for the master bedroom. All the plants used in the garden were authentic old varieties, preserved in the National Council for Conservation and Protection of Gardens Collections and in the Heritage Seed Library.

The second section of the garden was given over to a 'toy' vegetable garden, planted with broad beans, peas, lettuces and radishes. And then beyond that was a space where the Bowler family would later erect a hen coop.

The dining room and front parlour

The two principal downstairs rooms needed a thorough going over in order to be restored to their place as the public showcases of the house: rooms where the family would entertain and impress. For a start, all traces of the late 1970s decoration had to be removed. The effect of doing this was certainly spectacular, but, from a structural point of view, it was simple enough to accomplish. Most of the 70s additions – for all their obtrusiveness – were cosmetic, as, indeed, were most of the 1900-style renovations.

The ceilings of the two rooms were stripped of their polystyrene tiles and the plaster underneath made good and painted with white distemper. Happily, the ornate ceiling roses had been tiled around and were still intact, and the cornices were also unharmed.

The walls were stripped back. In the front room there was evidence, under the layers of paper, of a stencilled frieze. It was an attractive feature but Daru decided it was rather later than 1900 in date and distinctly Art Nouveau in style, the team decided that it must be covered up again. New picture rails were affixed. The rooms at once seemed to return to their intended proportions.

The close-fitting carpet was taken up along with several layers of old lino underneath it, to reveal the original floorboards below. These were coated with a dark wood stain, to improve their colour and help keep down the dust.

The flush hardboard panels that had been tacked on to the doors were taken off. Underneath the old panelling remained, somewhat knocked about but easily restored.

Below: *Despite the ceiling tiles, the radiator and the modern fireplace, the front room still retained something of its original character in the ceiling rose and cornices.*

Above: *A length of Art Nouveau frieze was uncovered in the front room.*

Right: *A period fireplace, with a hooded grate and a tiled surround, provided a distinctive focus for the room.*

Some very unfortunate reeded glass had been put into the upper frames of the connecting double-door between the two rooms. This had to be taken out and replaced with wood.

The fireplaces, too, needed radical surgery. The original ones had been blocked in and covered up. In the back room a little gas fire had been installed, and in the front a 1950s tiled grate. Both had to go. Among the in-fill behind the 50s fireplace the team found some smashed-up pieces of the original marbled fire surround – clues to how the old fireplace would have looked.

Having stripped out all the unsightly modern accretions, the process of building up the richly textured, patterned and coloured details of a 1900 interior began. In token of their importance the rooms were fitted with elaborate gas lights. There were still traces in the walls (and in the ceiling roses) of where the old fittings had been. Many fine old gaslights still survive, and can be picked up quite cheaply. But, due to the change in the pressure at which gas is delivered to the home, like the gas pipes, they are unusable without adaptation. Their mechanisms would be unable to cope with the modern supply. And, as Lia remarked, 'We wanted authenticity, but we didn't want to blow up half of Charlton.'

Although it is possible to have old lights refitted with new valves, for reasons of safety (and convenience) Lia resorted to a company that makes high-quality reproduction gaslights – principally for the pub and hotel trade.

The lights were fitted with 'incandescent mantles' which would have been the acme of advanced technology in 1900. By mixing air with the gas and passing through a treated gauze they were able to give off much more light than earlier, conventional 'batwing' burners, while at the same time using less gas.

The décor of the two rooms was built up layer by layer. The dining room was to serve a double purpose. Despite its name, it was used not only for dining but also for many of the activities of daily family life. As a result its décor had both to impress and be practical. It was,

Above: *Daru pots an aspidistra on the dining table. Only the hardiest house plants could survive the fumes and gloom of a 1900 room.*

Right: *A late-Victorian writing desk and blotter. Letter writing was one of the domestic activities that took place in the dining room.*

Below: *Lia assembled a collection of distinctive objects. Like a suburban family of the time, she was striving to create an impressive effect on a limited budget.*

perhaps, the former consideration that usually dictated the colour scheme. Rich dark colours were preferred. Daru searched through old pattern books to discover an appropriate wallpaper, and then Lia tried to match it. In the end, the rich dark-red and brown paper that she found was a modern design by Nina Campbell. But it had clearly been based on a late-Victorian model and, with its distinctive combination of swirling paisley motifs and broad stripes, had exactly 'the right look'.

The paper was hung up to the level of the dark-painted picture rail, then the upper part of the walls and the ceiling were painted white, providing some valuable lightness amid the prevailing gloom.

To maintain the sense of richness, oriental rugs were laid down on the dark floorboards. By a stroke of good fortune Lia found a pair of period curtains in a heavy brown fabric, already made up. They were in remarkably good condition and needed only minor alterations before they could be hung over the french window leading out into the back garden. An antique fireplace with a fake marble surround was installed in the chimney breast.

The furniture for the room all tended towards enhancing the air of substance. The table, sideboards and chairs were in dark wood with ponderous designs. Finding such items was not without its unexpected difficulties; 'It took me a while to get my eye in,' Lia confessed. 'I soon realised that if I liked the

Below: *The view from the dining-room through into the front parlour: the connecting doors would have been kept closed except on special occasions.*

look of anything it was almost certainly wrong – either too early, too late, or made in France.' Lower middle-class, late-Victorian taste was largely a matter of mechanically reproducing fashionable styles from a slightly earlier period. As a result it can look rather heavy and coarse. And this effect was in no way diminished by the late-Victorian habit of covering table and sideboards with tapestry cloth and covers.

The objects, like the furniture, were selected to project an image of established prosperity – the goal to which all middle-class families aspired. Lia even gathered together a selection of framed portrait photographs to provide the Bowlers with a ready-made set of ancestors.

Some practical considerations were also addressed in the furnishing of the room. As a supplement to the gas lighting several oil lamps were provided. (Again reproduction models were used for safety reasons.) The warm, bright light they give off is much better suited to some of the more intricate tasks – such as letter writing or mending – that would have been done at the dining-room table.

The rich dark tones of the dining room gave way to a rather lighter scheme in the front room – a room that, according to the nicely graded calibrations of middle-class vocabulary, would have been called the front parlour, the sitting room or the drawing room. For the walls Lia was able to find a bold yellow-on-yellow floral paper that Coles had been producing continuously since the late 1890s. Again this was hung only up to the level of the picture rail; the upper wall, ceiling and indeed the picture rail were painted white.

The bay window looking out on to the street was heavily veiled with three layers: wooden Venetian blinds, net curtains, and

Above: *Daru was surprised to learn that Venetian blinds were a prominent feature of 1900 décor.*

Below: *A* Punch *cartoon from 1900 showing a curtained fireplace.*

Mabel (stroking kitten, a new present). "MOTHER, ITTY'S SO HOT! OUGHT SHE TO SIT SO NEAR THE FIRE?" *(Kitten purrs.)* "OH, MOTHER, LISTEN! SHE'S BEGINNING TO BOIL

Above: *The draped and ornamented fireplace in the front parlour – the high altar of domestic life.*

then conventional green serge curtains set under a pelmet. Modern reproductions of old patterns were used for all three elements. Daru and the other members of the team were surprised to discover how prevalent

Above: *The front parlour in all its glory, its proportions re-established by the restoration of the picture rails.*

Venetian blinds were in 1900 décor, as can be seen in the photo of Elliscombe Road in 1900 (see page 32). 'We tend to think of them as a modern element,' he explained. 'But in fact most late-Victorian houses sported them, particularly on front windows. They were the main barriers against the light. The curtains proper were more for show.'

The Victorian enthusiasm for covering things up with swags of fabric extended even to the fireplace; this, too, was draped with curtains. This potentially hazardous procedure was recommended as a means of 'modernising' a room economically. The fireplaces installed by the builder–developer tended to be both cheap and old-fashioned. While it would have been expensive to install a new fireplace, the old one could be swept behind a stylish new curtain dressing for a rather more modest price. It was the common 1900 solution to most decoration problems. The modern view tends to be: if you don't like something, strip it out or paint it white. The late-Victorian approach was: if you don't like something, cover it up with something bright and flounced.

Even here, however, the practical side of the equation could not be ignored. Household guides of the period give strict admonitions that wool or serge should be used for fireplace dressings, as such fabrics would merely smoulder if they came into contact with a burning coal. Silk or satin would go up in flames.

The belief that the Victorians covered the legs of their pianos out of a sense of modesty may be apocryphal. But there is no doubt that the upright piano existed as an extremely important element in many middle-class homes of the period. It was a symbol of respectability and accomplishment, as well as a means of home entertainment. Lia was thrilled to find an excellent period model for the bargain price of £260.

The sofa too was a good find: a 1900 piece still with its original cover. After a hundred years the upholstery was getting a bit tired and lumpy, but the period feel was so 'right' that they decided to leave it unchanged. Whether – or how far – to restore antique items was one of the team's recurrent dilemmas. They did not want things to look too 'antiquey'. In 1900 the objects that now look old would have been brand new. A balance had to be struck. Part of the solution to the problem was to have two people working flat out for a fortnight cleaning all the period furniture with vinegar, beeswax and elbow grease, so that it looked 'nearer to new'.

Filling the front room with appropriate objects provided a succession of interesting challenges. The fireplace, beside its curtains, needed a great deal of additional paraphernalia – fender, fire screen, fireguard, fire irons. And, rising above them, was the three-tier mantelpiece. It was dressed to impress with decorative fans, figurines and vases of dried flowers. (Given that front parlours were used only on special occasions, dried flowers or indestructible pot-plants were preferred to fresh flowers.) The walls were adorned with conventional pictures – prints of flowers, animals and patriotic scenes.

Particularly interesting were the toys and games that Lia provided for the children. In an age before computers, television, or even radio, families had to make their own entertainment. Board games, puzzles and toys abounded. They still have a certain charm. Nevertheless Lia was concerned that modern expectations were higher and modern attention spans shorter. 'I'm sure I bought more toys and games than any family would really have had at the time. But I thought the children would get through them so much more quickly.'

The upstairs landing

The decorative scheme used in the hallway was continued up the stairs and along the landing. Rather than using linoleum on the floor, however, runners were put down on the bare dark-stained boards. The picture rail, too, was dispensed with. To give some light, in what was otherwise a very dark space, a bracket-shelf was erected on one wall to hold a small night light.

The built-in linen cupboard, at the top of the stairs, was the house's great archaeological treasure store. Although it was old, it had clearly been erected after the house had been

Above: *The girls' bedroom. Household guides of the period recommended blinds as well as curtains, to ensure uninterrupted darkness even on the brightest summer mornings.*

decorated. Inside were preserved traces of the original hall wallpaper, and also a length of the original dado rail. These internal features were left untouched, but the outside of the cupboard was painted with the same dark brown paint used for the skirting.

Stocking this linen cupboard with authentic period sheets and towels introduced the team to a whole range of forgotten fabrics and textures. It brought an immediate sensory element to the project: every new item felt different and distinctive. The variety of fabrics, too, was impressive: linen, flax, hemp, cotton and combinations of the same. Lia even discovered some sheets woven from 'nettle'. She decided against them, however, in favour of a set of hempen sheets that she found in France. Such sheets were once common in England too, but the quick pace of modernisation has carried most of them off by now. They are much more readily found – and cheaply bought – on the continent.

'They feel so different to cotton,' Lia enthused. 'They have a wonderful heavy texture.' Her only anxiety was that they might be rather unwieldy when it came to making the bed.

The 1900 bath towels that Lia found were even less familiar than bed sheets. They were flat-woven rather than tufted. She almost felt that she should label them as 'towels' so that the Bowlers did not mistake them for sheets or tablecloths.

The children's bedrooms

In 1900 the modern ideal of each child having a room of his or her own was just coming into focus. And as the size of the average family steadily declined and the size of the average family home steadily increased, the reality came nearer. In many families some siblings, near in age and of the same sex, continued to share bedrooms and even beds, but the dense crowding of earlier decades was largely avoided, at least by the middle classes.

Returning the two children's bedrooms on the first floor to a 1900 condition was relatively simple. No structural alterations were needed. The fireplaces, though boarded up, were still in place. The walls of the smaller room were painted with pink distemper, those of the larger one were papered. Light colours were used as these, according to late-Victorian thinking, gave less strain to the eyes. The team did consider covering the floorboards with a wash of potassium permanganate, a deep purple-brown disinfectant stain much used at the time. But in the event they opted for a more conventional floor stain, albeit of a similar colour. Rugs were put down beside the beds.

It was decided not to extend the gas lighting system up to the rooms on the first floor, despite the fact that there was evidence of gas piping in the walls. Even if there had been gas lighting upstairs at 50 Elliscombe Road in 1900, such a feature would have been atypical. There was a general prejudice against having gas lighting in bedrooms; it was thought to be a health risk. And the team's aim was to create a thoroughly typical suburban house.

Given that there was no gas (let alone electric) lighting in the room, and no WC or basin in the house, there were several specific demands placed on the furnishing and decoration of the bedroom. Tile-backed washstands were provided, the bowls of which could be filled with water from a ewer. And chamber pots had to be found to go under the beds. Both the pots and the washstand basins would have to be emptied daily. Some beautiful coloured cut-glass night-light holders were found in order to dispel the absolute darkness of the rooms at night.

The beds themselves were more familiar. Or, at least, they appeared to be. One of the iron bedsteads, having been carefully

PRESENCE OF MIND.

Little Girl (who has been disturbed by a Mouse, in a stage-whisper to her sleeping sister). "WAKE UP! OH, WAKE UP AND MEW, AMY, MEW FOR YOUR LIFE!!"

Above: *A* Punch *cartoon of 1900 showing that it was still conventional for sisters to share a bed even in middle-class households.*

Above: *The master bedroom before restoration. The original mantle piece had survived as a frame for the modern gas fire.*

assembled, promptly collapsed when one of the production crew sat on it. Close inspection revealed a small wing-nut upon which the whole bed-construction depended. Luckily, a ninety-degree turn was all that was needed to make the frame stable and secure.

Storage space was limited. In the larger of the two bedrooms there was a built-in wardrobe to the right of the fireplace. For the other room Lia found a bulky, mahogany chest of drawers and a trunk. She also provided both rooms with rows of pegs to hang clothes on.

The number of clothes that people had is one of the telling differences between life in 1900 and life now. A hundred years ago it was not uncommon for people to possess only three outfits: one for wear, one for the wash, and one for 'best'. As a result, even though clothes were rather bulkier than they are now, their storage was less of a dominant feature of home – and particularly bedroom – arrangement.

The master bedroom

The front room on the first floor presented an interesting challenge. The original plasterwork was missing. The ceiling was new, or – at least – new-ish, and it was lower than in the other rooms. It appeared to date from the late 1940s, and Peter suspected that it had been put in to repair bomb damage. Certainly a bomb had fallen in the area, taking out several houses in the street, and very probably causing much incidental damage.

Above: *The master bedroom after restoration. The late-Victorians had strong views about bedroom wallpaper, advocating patterns that were 'pretty yet unobtrusive'.*

To their surprise, however, when they took down the modern ceiling, they found the old one, intact, underneath it. 'It really is a bit of a mystery,' confessed Peter. 'Perhaps it was some sort of scam, and they had put in a claim for bomb damage compensation.' Whatever the reason, the discovery of the old ceiling simplified the task of restoration. The picture rail was missing, but it could be remodelled from examples existing in the other rooms.

Stripping back the walls revealed traces of the same Art Nouveau frieze that had been discovered downstairs. It was covered up again with a light, patterned paper. Lightness became the dominant mood of the decoration. The windows were decked with light floral curtains, as well as with nets and a Venetian blind.

The furnishing of the room – with a washstand, iron bedstead and chamber pots – was similar to that of the other bedrooms, although rather grander. The chamber pots were provided with pot lockers to keep them out of sight. One mirror was hung above the fireplace and another above the small chest of drawers. There was room, too, for a modestly sized wardrobe.

The bathroom

Number 50 Elliscombe Road has always boasted a plumbed-in bathroom. And 'boasted' is the operative word. The room would have been one of the major selling points of the original house. Such a feature was both a novelty and a luxury in 1900.

Although the position of the room – at the back of the first floor – has remained unchanged, the internal arrangement of the room had altered considerably over the century. A bathroom in 1900 was literally that: a room with a bath in it. The installation of a plumbed-in basin and WC were later additions. The bathtub itself had also been modernised.

In returning the room to its 1900 state all these modern fittings had to be removed. The original etched glass in the lower half of the window and in the door was still in place, and, although it had been painted over, the paint was easily stripped off.

The walls, ceiling and floor were stripped back and then treated as simply as possible to facilitate cleaning and to minimise the possibilities of mould. A varnished paper was used on the walls, its mosaic design suggesting the sort of treatment that might have been found in a more opulent bathroom. Ironically an equivalent paper would have been a penny a roll in 1900; it cost a hundred pounds a roll today. The floor was covered with the same chequered linoleum that was used in the kitchen, and the ceiling with the ubiquitous distemper.

Lia's network of salvage dealers provided a wonderful cast-iron sarcophagus-shaped bath with clawed feet. It was to be the only fixed feature of the room. The other large element called for was a free-standing, marble-topped, tile-backed washstand with a ceramic bowl and a water jug. Plumbed-in washbasins came very late to middle-class homes. Indeed the whole question of where one washed – at a washstand in one's bedroom, at a washstand in the bathroom, or over the sink in the scullery – was a matter of nicely graded social distinction.

Nevertheless, even here, practical imperatives would sometimes intrude themselves. Bathroom washstands, although fashionable,

Below: *The upstairs bathroom before restoration. The basin and the WC were both novel installations which would need to be removed.*

Opposite: *Plumbed-in basins were almost unknown in 1900. Tile-backed washstands, although labour-intensive, were the norm.*

Above: *The bathroom after restoration. The frosted glass in the bottom half of the window was an original feature.*

had their limitations. The etched glass commonly used in bathroom windows tended to make the rooms rather dark and, consequently, delicate operations such as shaving could become difficult, if not dangerous. Many a middle-class father ended up shaving at the scullery sink for the sake of the additional light.

Shaving, of course, was difficult enough already in 1900. Although Mr Gillette had just invented the first safety razorblade, most men continued to use the traditional cut-throat razor. An antique model, with a new blade, was found, much to the alarm of the Health and Safety inspector.

There was some anxiety, too, over the question of toothbrushes. In the pre-synthetic age, toothbrush bristles were made from hog's hair. Although Lia was thrilled to find a whole consignment of unused 1900 toothbrushes overlooked in an old warehouse, she became concerned about the potential health risk posed by the hundred-year-old hog's hairs. It was unknown how they had been treated. In the end she resorted to the replica model still made by Trumper's, the Mayfair barbers. Authenticity, it was conceded, must have its limits.

Such compromises, however, were rare. Number 50 Elliscombe Road had been returned to something very close to its original form. The front door stood ajar, leading back to 1900.

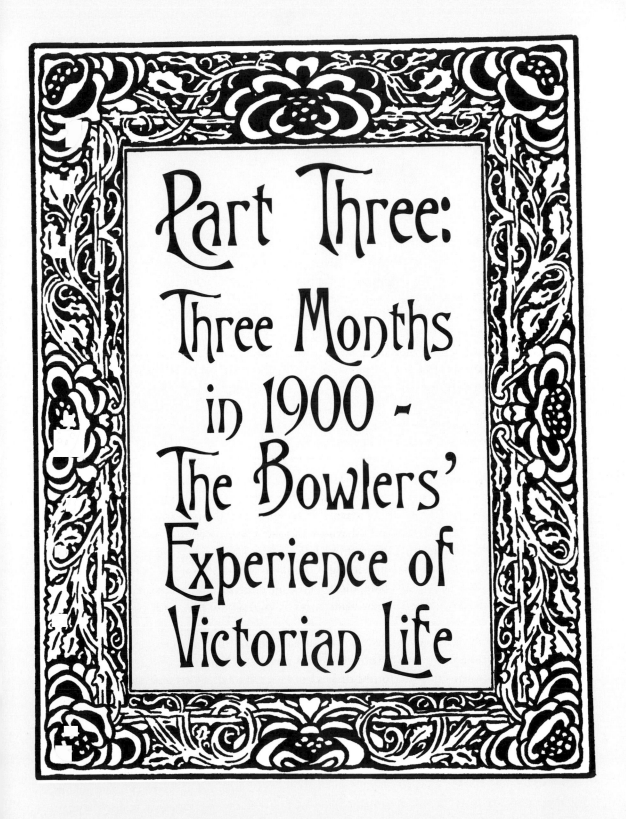

Part Three:
Three Months
in 1900 -
The Bowlers'
Experience of
Victorian Life

Raring 2 Go

'Why us?' wrote Joyce Bowler in her diary on the night her family was selected from over 400 others to take part in the 1900 House experiment. 'My mind is reeling. I can't wait to be the family in the 1900 House. I'm very excited, wondering if it's all a dream.'

Her husband Paul was delighted too. 'The most wonderful news,' he wrote. 'Yes, you guessed it, WE ARE THE 1900 FAMILY.' But he was also immediately thinking of the reality of what taking part in the experiment would mean. 'I am very excited, but the pressure seems to be on to get all the loose ends sorted out – i.e. schools for the girls, Joyce's job and even my work. I want the challenge for all of us, to grow as a family and as individuals.'

'Oh my God!' wrote daughter Kathryn, sixteen. 'I can't believe we have been chosen. I was so shocked I didn't know how to react. I have a million and one questions, but just forgot them all and started thinking about silly things like "Where will the chickens live?" and "Will we be on the front page of the *Gazette*?"'

The eleven-year-old twins, Ruth and Hilary, were told the news at their boarding school. Ruth was in the bath when her friend Amanda came running in, shouting, 'You and Hilary have won the television programme thing!' 'Everyone was really excited in our dormitory,' Ruth wrote in her diary later. 'And they were all telling us to mention their names.' 'I was shocked completely,' wrote Hilary. 'I had to sit down while all of my friends were congratulating me.'

A couple of days later and Joyce had sobered up a little. 'Of course it could all be a TERRIBLE MISTAKE,' she wrote. 'I spent most of Weds and Thurs with a silly grin on my face and then today I sort of "came down" and began to feel I'd imagined the whole thing. I feel like I did when I was pregnant, then had it confirmed but it was too early to go round telling people. Bizarre. It's like, "I know something you don't know."'

'I never did think of it as a costume drama,' she went on, 'so it's good to see that the TV company don't either. That would be a real fiasco with me doing a Mrs Bridges in the kitchen and Paul being – well his version of a Victorian male stereotype, I suppose. Now that wouldn't be a costume drama or even a comedy – it'd be a bloody tragedy.

'Driving home from work yesterday,' she continued, 'with Jimi Hendrix, Hipsway and Talk Radio on in the car, I had to turn everything off and just calm down. I love all this stuff about the costermonger and keeping to a budget and household accounts. I shall have to plan my menus and get back to cooking for all of us again. I do tend to live in my own fantasy world sometimes.

Now someone is allowing me to do it BIG STYLE!! It's legit!!' Only one thing nagged her. 'Should I go on a diet? Is it true that TV makes you look fat? Oh, who cares?'

As the days went on Joyce started to worry more. 'What if I let everyone down?' she confided to her diary. 'What if I can't get the water hot and breakfast ready and make packed lunches and buy the right things? What if the kitchen range doesn't like me? Suddenly I've got cold feet because it's all become a bit too real.'

Her main worry was how she was going to deal with being 'stuck in the house *all the time*'. 'Will it be my own little Victorian prison?' she mused. 'I do have a lot of freedom now and I use lots of strategies to stay sane and happy: 1) Music. Loud in the car, loud in the house (when next door neighbour is out – all I can disturb then are the pigeons and magpies in the field). 2) Dancing. At home and anywhere there's jungle drums and a space big enough to shake a leg. 3) Physical exercise. I don't run as often as I used to and now I'm feeling as if I really want to and I'll miss it. 4) Listening to the radio and talking to the people on it. The times I've had a barney with Tommy Boyd or Anna Raeburn and they haven't known about it! The point is, I'll have none of these things in the 1900 House. Will I go nuts?'

The practicalities continued to bug her, particularly how she was going to adapt to Victorian life as a vegetarian. 'Right,' she decided two days later. 'This is about a 1999 family living in 1900. OK, so they ate a lot of meat then, but we're not pretending to be them, are we? We're supposed to be us managing to survive under 1900 conditions. So we don't have to eat meat or boil up bones or any of those things.' As a vegetarian she couldn't cook meat. 'I certainly can't eat it. Part of me feels like we'll go vegan just to prove it can be done.'

Paul, meanwhile, had his own concerns. 'I need to find out if I should grow my facial hair,' he wrote. 'I have cleared it through the Regimental Major's, but I need to find out how much I ought to grow.' Of his wife he observed: 'Our whole conversation block is now on the house. Joyce seems to be taking on a heavy load. She thinks twice as fast as everyone else, right down to the *n*th degree. Then she comes out with a solution which is sometimes silly, but practical for her.'

Vegetarianism

'In the present day, when there are so many persons of really good position who, from conscientious grounds as well as those of health, restrict their food to vegetable diet only, it is of some importance to be able to serve a strictly vegetarian dinner.'

Vegetarianism in the late 1890s was something of a fad. It was enthusiastically promoted by George Bernard Shaw, and enthusiastically practised by many other 'persons of really good position'. Nevertheless it remained an object of suspicion, if not mild ridicule, to the majority.

There was a widespread belief that a vegetarian diet would sap the individual's constitution – and perhaps weaken the nation's strength. It was cautiously admitted as being 'suitable in certain cases, especially in dyspepsia and intestinal afflictions of a nervous origin'. And, of course, it was acceptable during Lent. One household guide of the period lists its vegetarian recipes under the heading 'Lenten and Vegetarian Dinners'.

A feeling persisted that vegetarian fare was, perforce, dull and worthy (a belief that persists to this day in some quarters). 'It will readily be admitted,' claimed one writer, 'that to give a vegetable dinner that will have the aspect of being hospitable is a matter of some difficulty.' The difficulty was made greater by the (supposed) fact that vegetarians are always strict teetotallers; 'and to finish up such a festive occasion with two decanters of cold water, and ask guests, "Which will you take – hard or soft?" instead of port or sherry, requires no little nerve on the part of the genial host'.

Nevertheless by admitting the use of cheese, eggs and even fish, it was possible to compose some passable, if uninspiring, 'Vegetarian Menus'. Popular dishes included coconut soup, cauliflower cheese, lobster salad, mushroom pie and turnip tops with poached eggs. For dessert, it was supposed, there could only be one choice: 'The Vegetarian is generally a great believer in dried fruits, dates, raisins, figs, & c. – he has them as a finish to every meal.'

Pasta was scarcely known. It appeared almost invariably as macaroni cheese, although Cassell's Book of the Household includes an interesting note on what it calls 'sparghetti', which it lists as a vegetable. The author suggested serving it with tomato conserve and Parmesan cheese, as an opening dish for a dinner, but added a coda. 'There is a famous little restaurant in Great Compton Street, London, known as the "Italian Café". If you want to have sparghetti to perfection, and see what it really is like before you try it at home, go there and ask for one portion; which will be enough for three ordinary Englishmen, but only sufficient for one Italian.'

Clothes not costumes

At the children's half-term the Bowler family took one step closer to their 1900 reality, getting up at 3 a.m. to travel up to Cosprops Theatrical Costumiers in London to be fitted for their costumes – or as Joyce insisted 'clothes'. 'I thought the corset would be a horrible constricting thing,' she told her diary that evening, 'but it was beautiful. It gave me a waist, decent posture, and it made me feel elegant and womanly. The undies are gorgeous! Especially the all-in-ones. To be wearing clothes of the period was such an honour. Actual clothes that women had worn in the late-nineteenth century. I couldn't stop staring into the mirror and it wasn't just vanity, it was to see a whole new me – a different woman looking back at me.' 'P.S.' she wrote at the end of that night's entry, 'I felt very ordinary when I was back in my 1999 clothes. Ordinary and drab.'

Below: *Joe Bowler with his favourite 'Victorian' toy: a wooden rifle his father made for him.*

Kathryn and the twins were equally enthusiastic. 'My clothes are fantastic,' wrote Kathryn. 'Especially the corset. I love dressing up and to wear beautiful clothes from a hundred years ago is such an experience. I felt like an excited little girl. I could tell Mum felt like that as well. She looked so elegant compared to her usual shirt and trousers combo. I really started to feel like a proper star this week,' she added. 'Everything was being organised around us and the reality started to set in. I felt so stupid when I was being filmed, though. Every time the cameras were switched on I became this very serious woman, who, instead of her usual blunt abusive statements, gave constructive criticism!'

Paul was pleased with his 'wonderful uniforms' and Joe's 'fab small boy's clothes', but made no further comment. He was more impressed with the behaviour of his children in front of the TV cameras. 'They were like stars,' he wrote. 'They talked and portrayed themselves as little adults. I have never seen them in this light before and I am so proud of them.'

Joyce had noted the change too. 'I don't want my family becoming big-headed,' she confided. 'We're special because we're us. Not because we're the 1900 family. It's going to be fun and a big adventure but the minute I spot anyone (including me!) looking in the mirror to see which is their "best" side, or practising signing their autographs – it'll be coats on, a brisk walk and "Let's get our priorities straight and remember who we are." Underneath all the fripperies like clothes and whizzing around London I mustn't lose sight of why I wanted to do this.'

In seventh heaven at Shugborough

The next item on the preparations agenda was a four-day trip to Shugborough Hall, a working Victorian stately home in Staffordshire, where the family were to meet a team of experts and be taught how to survive in their new – or rather old – surroundings.

In Shugborough's working Victorian laundry Joyce learnt how to remove stains with starch. 'A tip,' she wrote, 'which I will not only take back to 1900 but keep with me here in 1999. Could there be a resurgence in popularity of ordinary household starch? There is a movement away from the harsher detergents and things which pollute our environment. Does this herald a move back to more natural things? I doubt it. Some people may find it useful or interesting to use starch, but most people will go straight to the supermarket and buy the latest super-dooper instant remedy.'

Kathryn and the twins, meanwhile, were discovering how to iron the old-fashioned way. 'When you iron,' noted Hilary, 'you have to test to see if it's hot by flicking water at the bottom of the iron. Then you rub it on the spare material to clean it. Then you rub soap on a piece of cloth, then on to the iron.' She was enjoying all aspects of the new experience. 'I love being filmed,' she wrote. 'I was filmed washing some bloomers and that really hurt my back but I am OK now and I will get over it.' Getting to grips with the hard work involved had brought closer the reality of what they were all letting themselves in for. 'I am still up to going to the house,' she continued, 'but I think things are going to be very hard now I have tried them for real. I wish we could know more about the house. We know absolutely nothing. This is like a painful, funny mystery.'

Confronted with the reality of the Victorian kitchen, Paul was equally apprehensive. 'I am still concerned about the hazards we are going to face,' he wrote. 'The range, oil lamps, gas lamps. Are we going to have had enough preparation for the experience?' He was also concerned about the changes in his children. 'The girls are growing in confidence and manner. I worry about the star-struck image they can portray at times. I want them to understand that we are still the Bowlers and when we finish it will be work as usual.'

But Joyce's energy was unstoppable. 'I was in seventh heaven yesterday,' she wrote, 'being allowed to do what we've always dreamt of in a National Trust House, i.e. touching things, using things and playing with all the stuff. One of the ladies has a wonderful job dressing up and demonstrating techniques to school parties, giving them a taste of what life was like for the Victorians. That's what I'd like to do. Playing at dressing-up all year round and having an enjoyable time. It's like being three and never having to leave the home corner and the dressing-up box. Maybe I didn't play enough as a little girl or maybe I just never moved on or grew up!'

The next day found Paul and Joe up at seven to visit Shugborough's farm and learn how to look after chickens. The womenfolk, meanwhile, tried out the working Victorian kitchen, in particular the machine that would soon be the troublesome centre of their lives. 'The kitchen range was very impressive,' wrote Joyce. 'It belted out a lot of heat and the ovens were really effective. We managed to cook biscuits and a seed cake and I was really interested in the way the heat was controlled and the evenness of temperature.'

'The range looked fantastic when it was lit,' wrote Ruth. 'The flames were roaring and it was fascinating to see how you check the temperature and direct the flames. When we put in the biscuits it said for fifteen or twenty minutes, but as the fire was so hot we had them finished in about six minutes.'

'Can I manage this?' Joyce wondered later. 'We'll have to be economical with the coal. The range guzzles it up! My aim is to try and keep it in all night, so I'm really going to have to build up my knowledge and experience as quickly as possible. How much coal will we get? I don't think we'll be having fires in the bedrooms unless the children are ill or it's really bitterly cold. The kitchen range has first call on all the coal supplies!'

Paul foresaw a different problem. 'What we have done here in our twentieth-century clothes we will have to do later in our restrictive nineteenth-century clothes. It will take time and a lot of patience.'

'I really don't want to leave Shugborough,' wrote Hilary that night, 'because everything is so nice. I made some cool biscuits in the kitchen, it was way cool. Everything has been going so well. I am so excited I just want to go now. Now! I would love to go straight to the house.'

Glycerine and Gentleman's Relish

There were, however, a whole three weeks to wait before the Bowlers moved in. Three weeks to allow the novelty of the project to wear off and all kinds of doubts and fears to set in.

'Coming home,' wrote Kathryn, 'was the worst part of last week. I didn't want to face the reality of my tip of a bedroom, my piles of work, and the jobs that always need doing around the house. If Mum and Dad are like this when we're in the house, I'm going to have to up and leave. I'll become a suffragette and fight for women's rights! God – stardom is stressing me out. I've decided to become a "lovey" and retire after this documentary.'

'I'm finally beginning to see it as a reality,' wrote Joyce, 'and I'll be honest, it's a bit chilling.' She had told the film crew she was ready to go straight to the house. 'But maybe that was to stop me thinking, getting scared or changing my mind. Oh God, we're in it now for better or worse, what have I done?' 'P.S.' she added. 'Dusting yesterday with George Michael – how can I do housework without him?'

A couple of days at home restored her optimism. 'It's an adventure and I'm going to go on my adventure in a corset,' she wrote. Now she was actively planning.

'List of things I have just thought of:
1) Tweezers. Did Victorian ladies pluck their eyebrows at all? If not then we'll need them for splinters.
2) Sewing kit for repairs.
3) Rags for kitchen.
4) Umbrellas for wet outings.

'I may become quite houseproud,' she continued, at the end of a long catalogue of items, 'i.e. not wanting people with dirty shoes and boots to come tramping through my house! I think we'll have a strict rule about removing them at the door. Oh cripes!! I just made a STRICT RULE and I've been so dead against rules.' It was still the raw practicalities of the experiment that were intriguing Joyce. 'I'm not so interested in the being on TV, being recognised in the street, side of it. When it's televised I might try and pretend it's not happening, it's not me. Failing that I'll go for the posh dress and Sunday supplement interview.'

Was this true, however, of their neighbours and acquaintances? 'Sunday night,' Joyce wrote. 'So many people are saying that they want to come and visit us in the 1900 House. People who aren't particularly good friends, people who would never dream of visiting us ordinarily. At first I didn't mind and was saying, "Oh yes, you must come and see us." Now I'm wondering if it's us they want to see or just the house and we'll turn into a peep show. No, a freak show is more like it. I don't want to be a funfair attraction. Come and see the amazing Bowlers, five children and a wonderful line in corsetry. Roll up! Roll up! They sing! They talk to cameras! They light fires! They spend all flipping day washing their smalls! It's the highlight of the century – the amazing Bowlers. Wind them up and watch them go!'

Back at school, the twins were experiencing a similar popularity. 'Today everyone wanted to know about the television programme,' wrote Ruth. 'Friends, teachers, Matron.' 'My friends,' Hilary confided, 'keep telling me every day, "You are so lucky, oh, I wish I was you, etc."' Some of them were even getting in on the act through the girls' new diaries. 'I think this is a good opportunity for Hilary and Ruth,' Natasha Goatham (twelve) testified. 'I'm very pleased for them as I would love to be in their position right now. I wish them all the best.' Meanwhile Hilary could hardly contain herself. 'I AM RARING 2 GO!' she scrawled.

'I am becoming OBSESSED with all things Victorian,' Joyce recorded, back in Taunton. 'Everything I do I compare to how it might have been done in 1900. Cooking

Above: *The Bowlers arrive at 50 Elliscombe Road by authentic period horse and cart. At the front door Daru Rooke waits to greet them.*

and washing, of course, but I'm starting to read labels on produce to see when it was first in use. Today it was Gentleman's Relish and HP Sauce. Tomorrow I will scour the chemist's for old-fashioned face cream. Glycerine is a good find but I wonder if it was used on faces? Will I be all wrinkled and grey-haired by June?

'I am obsessed with the 1900 House. I think about it, I dream about it, people keep asking me to talk about it. I've got to the point where I DO NOT WANT TO TALK ABOUT IT. To be honest, I'm starting to dread it. I love my modern appliances. I need my washing machine. Is it going to be hell? Every little thing I do these days is becoming a point for deep thought – like turning off the light in the bedroom and putting on my bedside lamp. Will we have gas mantles in the bedrooms? Or just candles? Or oil lamps? We are going to have to be so safety conscious.'

Like Joyce, Paul had started to fantasise about his new home. 'I hope the house is what I think it's going to be,' he wrote. 'A small house with – I don't know what to say. All I can see is the cooking range and small wooden table with four chairs around it, gingham curtains over a Belfast sink and one tap. It feels like a survival exercise rather than an adventure.

'We are now talking,' he went on, 'about really nitty gritty stuff that means a lot to the individual, such as period towels for J/K/H and R and what sort of consequences that will have. I am not so worried other than that I will smell a little. But having gone for 10–14 days in the Arctic wastes you get used to your smell and that of everyone around you. It's only clean people who notice the difference.'

'This whole thing is bizarre,' Joyce wrote on the night before they left Taunton.

'Time-Travel Unlimited
Next expedition due to leave on March 14th 1999
Destination: London, England.
Time: Spring 1900.
Passports not required but stout boots and a corset are. A fear of hard work is
   not recommended.
Immunisations: None available at the time, so travellers must be willing to risk
   all and take it as it comes.
Costs: To be counted in many ways but not until the time-travellers return. May
   be in £.s.d. or in £ and pence, may be in personal terms.
Possible drawbacks: No mod-cons. No en suite facilities. Probably not suitable
   for vegetarians.

'Yes, as I said, bizarre.'

Moving in

The day had finally arrived when fantasy and expectation were to become reality. In the unfamiliar surroundings of the Clarendon Hotel, Blackheath, Paul had been awake since 3 am. 'Not knowing what is going to happen,' he wrote in his diary. 'I am ready. I feel strong inside to take my family back to 1900.'

Joyce woke at 6 am. How was she feeling? Paul asked. 'Terrified,' she replied. 'And excited too,' she wrote. 'Today's the day. I can't think straight. Must eat something, but I feel so odd that I wonder if I can actually manage to swallow anything. In a few hours I will have travelled back in time to the year 1900. Am I ready? No luggage! No packing!! We will step over the threshold and go from 1999 to 1900. Don't even have to bother with a time machine. The clothes are like a conveyance. Once they are on I feel very much the part, as if I am a Victorian. You just have to stand and move in such a way that it makes you feel very, very different to how you normally are. I can hardly write straight. I am fizzing inside. Let's hope I can retain a calm exterior and behave in a respectable manner as befits my 1900 counterpart later today.

Above: *Neighbours watch as the Bowlers enter their new home.*
Paul and Joyce had no idea what the house or street would look like.

Goodbye silly 1999 Joyce! Hello 1900 Joyce.' 'N.B. Boots *before* corset,' she scrawled hurriedly at the bottom of the morning's entry.

Paul, meanwhile, was worried about the white belt on his Royal Artillery warrant officer's uniform. How had they kept it clean in 1900? 'I must write to the Corps Museum, Eastney and ask,' he noted. Otherwise he was confident. 'We are a very strong family and will rise to any challenge given us. Our adventure begins. No more biro. Pen and ink from today.'

Hilary was thrilled with her family's new appearance. 'Our clothes are great,' she wrote, alongside a little sketch of the transformed family. 'We look very Victoriany. I love Dad's uniform. He looks so smart. I feel so excited. I would jump for joy but my boots are too stiff.' She had been saying goodbye to the twentieth century in her own way. 'I watched loads of TV before it gets taken away. Arrgh!'

Outside, it was, as Paul said, 'an absolutely beautiful day. We couldn't have asked for a better day.' In an authentic period horse and carriage the Bowlers left the Clarendon Hotel and proceeded at a trot across Blackheath Common and then down into the quieter backstreets of Charlton. 'I could feel myself

Below: *Social historian Daru Rooke. The Bowlers were pleasantly surprised by the lavishness of the house that they were to live in for three months.*

Lighting

The use of lighting in the home increased enormously during the last years of the nineteenth century. It has been estimated that there was a rise in domestic illumination of over 2000 per cent between 1855 and 1895. Most of this light was produced by coal gas. Candles were still used, but largely for their decorative effect. Oil and paraffin lamps remained popular; they were portable and inexpensive, and cast a pleasant light. The cheapness and abundance of British coal, however, ensured the pre-eminence of gas as a lighting source. In the late 1890s Londoners consumed 23,000,000,000 cubic feet of gas per year.

Gas was not a particularly efficient means of lighting – the flame tended to produce as much heat as light. But in the years before 1900 several innovations did much to improve this situation. In 1885 Count von Welsbach developed his eponymous incandescent mantle. Over the flame of the burner he suspended a small tube – or mantle – of muslin saturated with zirconia and other minerals. When the muslin was burnt, the minerals remained as a ghostly mesh; the flame burnt hotter and encouraged the carbon particles in the coal gas to become incandescent. More light was thus produced with less gas. Further improvements were made to this system throughout the 1890s.

Nevertheless certain disadvantages and dangers in the use of gas lighting remained. It was dirty and it smelt. It dried and heated the air. It consumed oxygen while 'producing sulphurous vapours' which rapidly destroyed leather and gilding. One household guide went so far as to assert that 'No one who had any regard for their decorations, hangings, or pictures will use gas in the reception room.' Yet, somehow, most people did.

The domination of gas was, however, being challenged throughout the period by electricity. Thomas Edison in America and Joseph Swan in Britain had developed the domestic light bulb, which had a filament within a vacuum, at the beginning of the 1880s. In 1881 they formed the Edison & Swan United Electrical Light Company to market their invention.

Despite the manifest virtues of electricity as a light source – cleanliness, safety, efficiency – and a general recognition that it marked the future, its actual spread into British homes was slow. Innate conservatism was partly responsible, and also economy. A new and expensive infrastructure of private power stations and power lines had to be put in place. But by 1900 there were thirty power stations in operation in London; many public buildings and the grander private houses had adopted electrical lighting. There were estimated to be over two and a half million electric lights in use in the capital.

As the new century advanced the yellow flare of gaslight rapidly came to be seen as one of the defining characteristics of the past Victorian age.

gazing around,' Paul said, 'at all the twentieth-century cars and buildings. But I was looking for something I could associate with – like a period house.' None of them had yet seen their new home. 'We didn't know which it was, so our heads were going left and right looking at the numbers, which side's even, which side's odd.'

At Number 50 Elliscombe Road they were met by a small crowd of locals; the TV crew, of course; and, perhaps most important, their adviser on all things turn-of-the-century, Victorian expert Daru Rooke, who had overseen the transformation of the house.

As they alighted, Daru was waiting for them at the front door and the family crossed the threshold into their new home. They were impressed. The house wasn't just beautiful, Joyce thought, it had a lovely atmosphere too. Paul was amazed at how rich he was. Daru had faithfully recreated the home of a Royal Marines' warrant officer of the period, 'and I was allowed,' Paul said, 'this magnificent house. It was better than I've got now, not just in terms of space – it looked luxurious, refined. We were expecting it to be much more downmarket.' 'I knew there would be knick-knacks around,' said Joyce, 'but some of the pieces were just so lovely – the china and the furniture. I hadn't expected it to be quite so lavish.' 'Totally spectacular,' was Hilary's verdict. 'Everything is so interesting. We can look around everywhere, touch everything – it's so homely.'

Daru then showed them round and briefed them on health and safety matters. With no electricity, 1900 was altogether a different and more dangerous world. Daru had given the family a start by lighting the fires and getting the range up and running.

When Daru and the others had gone, the Bowlers settled down for their first 1900 meal, cooked by Joyce on the range: eggs and fried potatoes followed by scones, cream and jam. 'Which was lovely,' confided Hilary to the video concealed in her bedroom cupboard. 'Everything is great here apart from the wallpaper in Mum and Dad's room, which is not cool at all.' 'It's really *sad*,' added her twin Ruth.

Night one and Joe wasn't missing anything. 'Just electric lights. I'm not really missing the computer or

Above: *Joyce cooking on the range. The Victorian 'heart of the home' was initially a source of endless trouble for the Bowlers.*

Pens

By late-Victorian times the feather quill had been comprehensively superseded by the steel-nibbed pen as the common writing instrument. The pens – or at least the nibs – were for the most part manufactured in Birmingham. Refinements in metal production and in design had, by 1900, led to a more flexible and accommodating nib.

Nevertheless writing with such a pen was a difficult business. Sudden splodges of ink were not uncommon, and blotting paper often had to be used to take off excess ink and prevent smudging. And, of course, the pen had to be dipped at regular intervals into an inkwell or bottle.

Constant efforts were made to overcome this last problem. Attempts were made to modify the form of the nib so that it could carry more ink. More successful were the efforts to invent a pen with its own 'reservoir' of ink. The earliest prototype fountain pens date from the mid-nineteenth century (there was even an experimental 'fountain quill') but it was not until 1884 that the American inventor, L.E. Waterman, produced the first commercially viable model.

Refinements in the design of the fountain pen continued during the first part of the twentieth century. Early models had to be filled up with a glass dropper; by 1911 the safety propelling model, with its own rubber sac for the ink, had been introduced. Ink cartridges came later.

By 1900 there were already several early versions of the ballpoint pen on the market, but they were unreliable and expensive. It was not until Lazlo Biro, a Hungarian journalist working in Argentina, developed his model in 1939 that the ballpoint pen began to supplant the fountain pen.

Opposite: *Paul being very careful with his cut-throat razor. To start with, it took him over half an hour to complete a shave.*

the TV – though I always like a TV. I've got games and lots of different toys. Soldiers, guns, chalk, lots of dolls, knights in armour...'

Joyce, meanwhile, having cooked the family dinner on the range, was trying to get to grips with another bit of 1900 technology. 'This ink pen is hell,' she wrote (splodgily) in her diary. 'How did Charles Dickens write such long books? My "Little Dorrit" would have been a "Minuscule Dorrit". What has today been like? Weird and wonderful. My thoughts are running so fast and this pen is holding me back. I need to slow down.'

But the day had been 'wonderful'. 'I just feel very comfortable here,' she told her video diary, 'it's just lovely. It just feels very natural really, to be here and be dressed like this. The corset returns your shape. I've had one of the best days of my life and now I'm going to go to sleep and start all over again in the morning.'

Paul was up early. At 6.15 am he was getting down his thoughts in his diary while waiting for the water to boil on the range. 'Yesterday was exciting, fantastic and a step back into 1900,' he wrote. 'Yes, we are the Victorians. It doesn't feel strange. It is as if we were meant to live here.' But already he, like Joyce, was feeling an enforced change of pace. 'Our way of doing things has to slow down. We have to be deliberate in what we do, as one thing interacts with another. Such as waiting for water for washing – and then who gets washed first? Does Joyce wait till we've all gone to sort herself out for the day?'

Having finally extracted a cup of tea from the range, Paul had his first 1900 shave – with a cut-throat razor. He had already taken instruction in how to do this at Trumper's famous barber shop in Mayfair. Now came the reality. 'I had forgotten how to change my wrist round,' he wrote later, 'to shave my neck properly. It was very frightening and I did it with extreme caution. I did succeed eventually and went away with a smoothish face.' But only smooth-ish. As the days went on he was to find that there was no way his shave would be as close as a modern one. He came to the conclusion that Victorians just wouldn't have been as well-shaven as contemporary men.

A Range of Frustrations

———◆◆◆———

onday was the family's first full day in the 1900 House and there was a huge amount to get used to. Cleaning your teeth with bicarbonate of soda; washing your hair with soap; cooking on the range; heating water for washing in the copper; washing up with soda crystals; deliveries to the door by the local butcher, baker and milkman – quite apart from detailed instruction in how to use oil lamps and gas mantles, stringent health and safety checks, and the filming.

'A *very long day*,' Joyce wrote in her diary that evening, 'which leaves me drained.' To the video in her bedroom cupboard she was more revealing. 'I'm feeling really negative tonight,' she confessed. Earlier, she continued, she had felt like running away. 'I felt stir crazy, as if I was trapped, imprisoned in the house. Perhaps I'm getting withdrawal symptoms from the twentieth century. I'd like to buy some washing-up liquid, and some shampoo, and some hand cream, and some face cream, and possibly some of that stuff you take on holiday to wash your clothes in, quick wash stuff.'

Next door in the girls' room, however, Hilary was still delighted with the whole experience. 'Ruth's asleep,' she whispered to her video diary, 'Joe's asleep and Mum's going to sleep, so I'm here by myself. I thought I might do a bit of a diary with my hates and my likes. My likes would be the food, the food is lovely, didn't think it would be this nice. My dislikes would be not knowing where everything is, because it's new all the time.' The toothpaste, she added, was 'revolting'.

For Paul it had all been 'quite stressful'. He had wanted to be left alone to get on with it all; to move things around to where *they* wanted them. 'Instead of which an army of people will walk in and try and film you doing it, and then they walk out and I have to clean up

Above: *Joe's first impression of the house and garden. The nine year old didn't keep a written diary, but did draw a few pictures of his 1900 life.*

Above: *Joyce prepares a vegetarian meal in the kitchen. In 1900 such a diet would have been regarded as an object of suspicion, if not mild ridicule, to the majority.*

again.' And the hot water in the range was a major disappointment. 'It's just not coming through, so we are having to boil loads and loads of water every time we want to go for a wash.'

By the second day, Kathryn had given up on her written diary. She was depressed, she said. 'It's hard, I don't know why. I'm very tired every day and I just want to go to bed. It's like being in the house all the time and knowing that you can't really go out and do what you want because there are so many restrictions. It gets me down.' Her feelings about her corset had changed, too. 'It's just so tight, it's very restrictive, I can't relax. I was tired yesterday afternoon so I thought I'd go and lie on my bed. I lay down,

Cooking

The coal-fired range was the chief means of cooking in British kitchens for the 150 years between 1770 and 1920. Its success was a result of Britain's large, cheap and easily transportable supplies of coal, rather than its conspicuous virtues as a cooking machine. During the period some refinements were made to its design. The fire gradually became more enclosed and the flues within the range became more complex. Less heat went up the chimney and more was used to heat the ovens, hotplates and water tank.

Despite these improvements the range still had its limitations. It was dirty, temperamental and time-consuming to use and maintain. In the later years of the nineteenth century the range was increasingly challenged by the gas cooker. There had been experiments with gas-cooking from as early as the 1820s, but a stubborn prejudice maintained against it. It was thought that the gas – which smelled unpleasant – would affect the flavour of the food. Also it was regarded as dangerously explosive, and expensive. Even with improvements in the design of gas cookers and independent gas-rings, and the introduction of a penny pre-payment slot system, the advance was slow.

It was not until after the First World War, when easy-to-clean enamel cookers were introduced, that the conspicuous benefits broke through consumer resistance. By that time electric cookers – which had begun to appear around 1900 – were also gaining in popularity. The two methods have advanced in tandem, developing temperature control devices, grill attachments and oven timers. The current trend is for cookers to combine both modes: the electric oven with the gas hob.

The microwave oven, which uses high-frequency radio waves, was not introduced into Britain until 1959.

I was completely stiff, completely uncomfortable and I wished I could rip the corset off and bung on a pair of jeans and a fleece – but this is the way it has to be.' It turned out that she was ill. The next day the doctor visited and diagnosed a minor case of flu. She was given some Gees linctus as medicine.

The twins, meanwhile, were making preparations for their mother's birthday – the following day, Wednesday 17 March. 'We're going to be making a little cake or something,' confided Hilary. Their presents were authentic to the period. Ruth was making a cross-stitch pincushion and Hilary had painted a small watercolour. It was all fine until Joe – painting his own birthday picture – spilt water all over Hilary's. 'I'm really upset,' she confided to her video diary. 'Now I've got to close the door,' she went on, 'because I'm talking about another issue. Mum and Dad have been shouting a lot at each other because they can't work things out. If they don't just grow up I don't know what we're going to do, because they've been told everything and we haven't. We don't know where everything is and they do. This place is like hell,' she added. 'Seriously, I just can't stand it.'

What were Joyce and Paul arguing about? 'Some things that matter we haven't got,' Paul said succinctly. Joyce elaborated: 'I'm bloody fuming about the little things that matter that we haven't got, and I'm not talking about twentieth-century things, I'm talking about 1900 things. I've got one dish cloth, one manky smelly dishcloth, which when I arrived was dirty. The copper doesn't work properly. The range isn't working: the heat exchanger isn't going properly and that's because we're using the wrong fuel; I mean even a novice like myself can tell it needs coal, illegal coal, because that's what it's built for, we're just not getting the heat with anthracite.' She felt overwhelmed by the hurdles that had been put in front of them. 'Such an enormous impact straight away. It's been bang straight into it. Culture shock.

'Everything is filthy,' she went on. You go into museums, National Trust properties and you see these beautifully laid out things, and frankly it's almost like a photoshoot for an interior design magazine.' It wasn't like that in reality, not at all.

She was starting to think that the Victorian housewife probably needed her daily trip to the shops, to see other people, because otherwise she'd have been a prisoner in her own home. 'Cleaning, you know, top to bottom, and bottom to top, and you know the minute you'd finished you start again. You'd be on a circle of cleaning.'

Joyce had also been looking though Mrs Beeton's cookbook, at 'all the fancy recipes and

Above: *Paul helps Joyce wash her hair, 1900 style. An infusion of egg yolk and lemon was one of number of treatments Joyce tried.*

suggestions', and wondering whether people had really lived like that. 'I mean I buy *Good Housekeeping* every month and half of it is packed full of wonderful ideas for, you know, your buffet party or your cooked lunch Perhaps at Christmas I might make something, but the rest of the year I just read them and look at the pictures and think, "Oh, that's great." A hundred years from now somebody could come across those magazines and think that they are representative of now; that we ate all this wonderful food all the time.' So she was coming round to the idea that the Victorians probably ate a very limited diet. 'They ate what was in season, what they could store and what wouldn't go off.'

The thing that was bugging Joyce most, though, was her hair. That morning she and the girls had tried Pears soap, but though the twins were happy enough, it was no good for her. Later she had dreamt up the idea of grating the soap and whisking it into a shampoo (with vinegar in the final rinse water), but that hadn't worked either. Now she felt terrible – 'just awful'. Her hair was all greasy and stiff. 'And I'd hoped it was going to be all lovely for my birthday tomorrow, but it's actually vile. Perhaps this is what Victorian ladies' hair was really like. Perhaps that's why it was always tied up out of sight. It doesn't look too bad in the photographs, but it must have been disgusting to touch, it must have been slimy and horrible.'

Paul was still deeply worried about the range. 'There must be something wrong with it,' he told his video diary. 'It just kicks out so much heat into the kitchen, the actual grate is so hot, but the water isn't warm, just slightly off cold. And trying to make a cake for Joyce's birthday for tomorrow, it didn't work. It didn't rise, it was in there for about two hours, for something that should have been in twelve minutes. We've had a baked potato in there, too, as a trial. I think it's been in there about six hours now and it still hasn't cooked. I want to get it right, because if the range isn't right, everything else is second place. Forget your pretty pictures, forget your curtains or ornaments, the main heart of the house is the range.'

A birthday dilemma

In the morning Joyce had cheered up thoroughly. 'Good morning,' she said, 'it's my birthday, I'm forty-four, and I've got a confession to make. Yesterday when I went over to see our neighbour Ruth across the road, as I was passing through her kitchen to go out into her garden to see her frogs, I couldn't help but notice she had a dishwasher, and I touched it. So that's my confession for today. But I think there are going to be some mighty big confessions coming up soon. I haven't done anything yet but I've got plans, revolving round the old barnet.'

'My biggest dilemma (yes there are others not quite so large),' she wrote in her diary a little later, 'is concerning whether I cheat so early on and get some shampoo. Kathryn and I are feeling rather anxious about going out in public with filthy hair. Sticky, soapy, filthy hair. I am so used to having my daily – even twice daily – shower and always washing and conditioning my hair.'

Otherwise the birthday went well. Paul brought Joyce breakfast in bed – he had managed to cook toast and boil eggs on the useless range, even if the milk had gone off and she had to have black tea. She loved her presents from the girls. Joe gave her three chickens – Patricia, Fortnum and Mason – and a cockerel called Charlie, which were delivered to the house by Fred Hams the chicken man. (Paul was building them a coop, as his present.) Kathryn had recovered, so Joyce went out shopping with her daughters. The range eventually warmed up enough to bake a cake, which was decorated by the children. Apart from a misunderstanding between Paul and Joyce about some burnt rhubarb, the day had gone wonderfully.

But as she headed up to bed that evening Joyce realised she had coal dust on her nightie. 'I can't wear this to bed,' she complained to her video diary. 'It's covered in coal. I was going to wear it all week. Where have I got all this muck from? This place is filthy, I don't know how anyone in Victorian times managed to stay clean. Your head gets full of coal dust, your clothes get covered in it, your skirts sweep along the floor. How anyone had any time to think higher thoughts, do philosophy, write books or whatever! It would have had to have been either a wealthy man or lady with servants, or somebody who didn't give a monkey's whether she had coal dust down her nightie.

Above: *Kathryn mops the kitchen floor while her mother prepares dinner. The amount of housework involved in 1900 life turned Joyce into a latter-day suffragette.*

'I think in actual terms,' she went on, 'the Victorian lady, even with a servant, would have just confined herself to the main living areas. Hall, stairs, so if anybody came off guard it looked good. Then the public rooms would be kept presentable, so that if Lady Muck or the vicar's wife turned up you've got somewhere for a nice cup of tea. And out in the scullery, who knows what was out there? Some poor soul labouring over two days' dirty dishes in a bowl of lukewarm water full of horrible washing soda crystals. I nearly spent my emergency twenty pounds today on washing-up liquid – isn't that awful?

'When we talk about the technology that we've got now at our fingertips, so many labour-saving devices, with lots of people it's almost like an inverted snobbery: "Oh I don't need to use that," they say. "We'll manage without that" – as if they're superior in some way. But now I think: "Why not have the best vacuum cleaner, why not have a super-dooper washing machine?"

'I won't pretend that I've got the presence of the Victorian lady who lived in this house hanging over me, or that I've had spirit messages or anything like that, but if it was me a hundred years ago and I was looking at somebody here now, I'd be saying: "Use it! This is what we prayed for, this is what we hoped for, for all those years. When we sat and read the suffragette pamphlet that somebody shoved through the door, before we threw it on the fire, before our husband saw it, that's what we were thinking of – the women of the future!" To think that it's only this century we got the vote and women still don't get equal pay for equal work in many parts of society. Women still have a long way to go. Maybe in a hundred years a woman will sit here talking into her diary – or whatever way they communicate then – and she will be looking back and saying, "Joyce knew there was something else, but she couldn't quite identify it." In just the way that my 1900 woman knew that there must be something better for her sex but she couldn't quite identify it.'

Oblivious to all this, Paul was worrying about the next day, when he had to go back to work, and the children were off to their new schools, and Joyce would be all alone in the house. 'I want her to be happy with everything that is going on,' he said, 'so that she can actually get on with it. I know she's a bit concerned about her hair. As long as you feel clean that's two thirds of the way there. Clothes as well. I've been scrubbing floors and I'm a bit worried about whether I smell or not.'

His shaving was proving an ongoing problem. 'It took me half an hour to shave today and I have got a few cuts here and there. I'm still not sure how to do my top lip. But the real problem is not the sides, but just round the bottom of the chin area. I was told to pull the skin up and over, but I tend to get the skin across – then I'm scared of slashing the bottom of my chin off.' In an effort to improve his technique he sat up late studying Cassell's *Book of the Household*, which was full of advice about all things Victorian from *How to Shave* to *How to Give a Dinner Party* and even how to be *The Master* of the house.

Beards

Although moustaches were considered more fashionable in 1900, beards still enjoyed some popularity, not least for their health-giving properties:
'In men throat-affections occur chiefly and, it is said, almost exclusively, amongst those who do not wear a beard. It is the opinion of many medical men that the beard not only adds materially to the general health and comfort of the individual, but is a powerful agent in prolonging life. It is said that amongst the records of the older medical writers there are few references to diseases of the throat, and that this is attributable to the then almost universal custom of wearing a beard. This may be true, or it may not; but at all events, if you habitually suffer from sore throat, our advice is, grow a beard if you can.'
The Family Physician

Victorian packed lunch

Getting the children off to their new schools in this strange new city had been, Joyce told her video diary the next morning, 'horrendous'. They had left the 1900 House in Victorian clothes, but then gone over the road to neighbour Ruth's to change into twentieth-century gear before setting off for their first day at the new schools. 'I think my son is going to hate me forever,' she continued. 'It's heartbreaking, doing what I had to do this morning. I've never seen him that distressed, I don't know how I'm going to make amends. Paul and I, we're big and ugly enough to look after ourselves, but I can't have my babies upset to that extent. I began to wish I could just take everybody back to how it was.'

Still, looking on the bright side, the range was working, and she'd made herself a pot of tea. 'I might even eat one of those Bath buns. Everything is peaceful and actually the house is wonderful, to be here on your own.' She had been going round the rooms pulling back the bedclothes, opening the windows, airing the place. She was beginning to feel that the troubles of the last few days were fading into 'teething problems'. They were starting to get things in their right places. They were learning some shortcuts too. 'I'm not wearing any drawers. Quite

frankly a Victorian wouldn't have had this amount of skirts on. She might have done if she was going for a special occasion – but it's going to save so much washing.'

    Above: *Paul returns from work in his Warrant Officer's uniform. When he travelled on the Underground to Kensington, 'nobody batted an eyelid'.*

    Ten minutes later she was back in the bedroom again. 'I just want to come upstairs and sing Glory Hallelujah, because we've got hot water in the pipes and it's only half-eleven. It's bloody marvellous! I've been downstairs saying thank you to the range. She's getting on a bit, you know, she's a bit of an old girl, but she's all right.' Now, armed with a brush and a broom and a bucket, Joyce was, she said, going to start at the top and sweep through, 'and hopefully by lunchtime I should be on top of things'.

    'The school's really nice,' said Ruth, when they'd all returned that evening. 'And we've got loads of good friends, so that's really, really good. Fantastico!' And, at lunchtime, both the twins had managed to stick to their Victorian packed lunch – cheese, apple and water – and resist the temptation of the 'loads of modern stuff' their new friends were eating. 'When they handed round the crisps I was being loyal to the programme and saying no.' Joe had a good day too. Kathryn's college, however, was not as she expected it to be, 'all strange and new and I'm missing my old college – which I never thought I would.'

    As for Paul, he had gone into work at the Royal Marines Careers Centre in Kensington High

Above: *Paul lights the fire in the back parlour. The family found they only used the formal rooms for special occasions.*

St on the tube, dressed in his 1900 warrant officer's uniform, 'and nobody batted an eyelid'. 'I think people did look,' he told Joyce,' but there are so many strange things going on in London, that they just thought, you know, "There goes another one," and walked straight past.'

The family had spicy lentils and potatoes for their evening meal, something that normally would have taken Joyce twenty-five minutes to whip up, but on the range took an hour and a half to prepare. Afterwards Joyce and Paul settled back into what Joyce described in her diary as 'a relaxed Victorian evening'. 'Not a lot happens. Me sewing, Paul sitting, watching along.' Joyce was starting to feel at ease with her new surroundings. 'I'm getting quite used to walking around and going into rooms where there aren't any lights on and feeling around chairs and things and going upstairs with candles into the gloom. It's not as unnerving as you think it's going to be.'

An awful confession and a dreadful row

Nonetheless, in the morning, the family had a huge row, the worst they had ever had, according to Joyce. It ended with the children refusing to go to school, the family saying they would pack in the whole 1900 project and Simon Shaw, the series producer, arriving to sort out everyone's differences. It had started with a subject close to Joyce's heart – shampoo.

Unbeknown to Paul, when Joyce had gone to the Co-op with the girls on her birthday she had cheated on the rules of the house and bought some modern shampoo. They had been being so good, just buying the 1900 things, packet tea and soda crystals and so on. But there was a two-for-one offer on shampoo and conditioner, and seeing those wonderful twentieth-century lifesavers right before her eyes, it had been, for Joyce, 'temptation beyond endurance'. 'We walked round a few times, then we came back to it, and I put it in the basket. And when Kathryn and I got to the checkout we thought that the chap in the till was going to know we aren't allowed this. But he didn't, he let us buy it and we felt like we'd smuggled something through customs. It was like, "Quick, put it in the handbag." So we sneaked it into the trusty handbag and got it home, at which point I realised I had two plastic bottles, so I decanted them – shampoo and conditioner – into some beautiful Victorian-style glass bottles with cork lids and we all washed our hair. We were riddled with guilt, it was almost as if somebody was watching us do this terrible thing.

'Then I was left with my two bottles of beautiful Victorian, so-called "hair preparation", but I also had two empty plastic bottles. So I put on Paul's dressing-gown

Below: *Joyce confides in her video diary. Apart from hidden safety features, the two cameras were the only modern technology in the house.*

Teeth cleaning

Toothpaste was unknown in 1900. Teeth were cleaned with toothpowder or 'dentifrice' as it was called. Although, by the end of the century, there were some ready-made patent brands on the market, such as 'Rowlands' Odonto' ('whitens the teeth, prevents decay: no grit nor ruinous acids'), the common expectation was that a household would prepare its own. The recommended recipes make rather alarming reading: one suggests a mixture of precipitated chalk, pulverised saponis, oil of eucalyptus and carbolic acid; another proposes combining precipitated chalk with borax, powdered orris root, bicarbonate of soda, and attar of roses. A more economical and more easily prepared recipe consists of nothing more than a piece of well-browned toast powdered up as finely as possible. Ground charcoal and chalk were also allowed, although it was admitted that neither was 'very pleasant to use'.

As ever, opinions varied on the question of the softness (or otherwise) of toothbrushes and the preferred direction of brushing. The hard, the medium and the soft bristle all had their advocates. Spon's guide favoured brushing away from the gum, while Cassell's prescribed not only an up-and-down action but a round-and-round one as well.

Morning and evening brushing was considered adequate, although several authorities also recommended rinsing the mouth after meals, using 'lukewarm water, in which have been sprinkled a few drops of toilet vinegar or eau de Cologne'.

and under cover of darkness, trotted out to use next door's bin. But it was sod's law really, because as soon as I got there the chap next door came home and caught me in the dark, putting something in his dustbin – it was a nightmare.'

When Paul found out about this, he was upset. If they were going to do this 1900 thing at all, he said, they should do it properly and stick to the agreed rules. What was the point of the experiment if they started cheating in the very first week? But the children didn't want to go to school with dirty hair. What would their new friends think? If they were going to have to go with dirty hair, and get teased, they weren't going to go.

'Oh God it was a nightmare!' said Joyce later. 'It was a battle of wills.' In the end, with Simon the producer adjudicating, the family reached a compromise. The girls could wash their hair in twentieth-century shampoo when they were out of the house, at the same time as they changed for school over at neighbour Ruth's. But Joyce was going to stay faithful to 1900, chucking out the beloved modern toiletries and using period hair-cleansers only.

Later, she admitted she had been wrong. 'It was terrible,' she confessed to her video diary, 'it was temptation and I strayed, I'm sorry. I didn't realise how important it was going to be to me, just to feel my hair clean and know that it wasn't full of coal and soap.'

Paul, too, was contrite. 'I am a bit of a bull in a china shop sometimes,' he wrote in his diary, 'not understanding others' feelings and expecting them to be and feel the same as me.' But the 'mare' had cleared the air. They were back on track, he reckoned. 'It's lovely to be here.'

Kathryn, however, hadn't enjoyed the family fight at all. 'There was a lot of shouting, banging, running up and down stairs,' she told her video diary. 'I hated it.' That morning she had had her first letter, from her best friend Sharon, whom she had been missing 'dreadfully'. She had been waiting for it for days. 'I just wanted someone to write to me. Everyone else is getting post and it was like: *Somebody write to me please.* And the day I got it, I come downstairs to eat my breakfast and read my letter quietly and all I get is shouted at.'

But even though the rest of the family had been threatening to abandon the project and leave, Kathryn was still keen to stay. 'We chose to do this and I wanted to do this and I really don't think leaving now would be the best thing. We've got to stick it out, and if we can stick out three months of hell, then I'm sorry, I can stick to anything. Throw anything at me and I reckon I can challenge it – because this is hell. I could never have been a Victorian.'

Ruth was equally low. She thought it would be best if they solved the whole problem of education by having a tutor in the house. 'At school it's really annoying because there's a load

of friends asking about our project and I don't really want to tell them. And then they say "Did you watch this on the telly?" and "Have you got that on your computer?" and I can't do those kind of things at the moment.' But

Above: *Hilary takes her potty to the outside toilet. The children rapidly adjusted to the gritty realities of Victorian life.*

she still loved the house. 'It's just not working very well, that's what I'm trying to say.'

Hilary, fortunately, was as sanguine as her father. 'We had a bit of a row this morning about being clean, and actually staying here, but it's all sorted now.' Now she had found a flyer from a local pizza firm which had been pushed through the door. 'Yum! So we're going to order a pizza,' she fantasised. 'I will have for my starter a 7-inch cheese and tomato pizza, and then for my main course I will have a deluxe Domino's classic pizza, and for dessert I'll have profiteroles, say five cream profiteroles served with dark chocolate sauce. And for a drink I would like a bottle of Coke. And all that would be, let's add it up, £13.13p, fantastic. Seriously, when I get back home I'm going to order a pizza, I'm going to have a mad feast of food, it's going to be so cool.'

House cleaning

Dust was the great enemy in the 1900 household. The coal-fired range, the coal-filled grates, the thick carpets and plentiful drapes conspired to create dust and then to retain it. Dust harboured germs, harmed fabrics and irritated noses. Against this foe the late-Victorian housemaid was armed with an impressive battery of brushes: there were banister brushes, stove brushes, carpet whisks and numerous other specialised creations. Yet all of these did little more than stir up the dust and redistribute it about the house.

Carpets could be taken outside and beaten, but this was a time-consuming and tiring operation, involving the complete re-ordering of a room's furniture. Finding an effective method of sweeping up dust became one of the grails of late-Victorian invention.

During the second half of the century some progress was made on this front. A range of carpet sweepers was developed. The most successful was the creation of Melville Bissell, an American inventor from Grand Rapids, Michigan, who named his model after his home town. The 'Grand Rapids' became enormously popular on both sides of the Atlantic; its heirs are with us still. The essential principle of a cylindrical brush revolving in a cased chassis mounted on wheels remains unchanged, although the introduction of ball bearings into the mechanism during the early 1900s certainly improved its running.

Separate from the development of the brush-based carpet sweepers, work was done on creating a cleaner that would use air either to suck or blow dust off surfaces and into a receptacle. Patents for such devices date back to the late 1850s, but the effectiveness of these early machines usually foundered on their inadequate power sources; the fan was driven either by the action of the machine's wheels – as with the carpet beater – or by a hand pump.

Real progress was not made until 1901. It was then that H. Cecil Booth, an English engineer, developed his proto-vacuum-cleaner. It was a vast contraption, looking more like a horse-drawn fire engine than a domestic appliance. It was powered by a 5-horsepower piston engine which could be run on either electricity or petrol. It could be summoned for special spring cleaning duties. The engine would be drawn up outside a household, hoses with specially designed nozzle attachments would be run up through the windows of the house by a troop of cleaners (all men, in the uniform of the British Vacuum Cleaner Company) and the dust sucked up and off into the cylindrical body of the machine out in the street. The procedure – and its effects – were highly dramatic. Some Edwardian hostesses arranged tea parties so that their guests might witness the event at close quarters.

The development of a portable machine for easy domestic use happened on the other side of the Atlantic. James Murray Spangler, an asthmatic janitor from Ohio, made a small, electrically powered, hand-pushed machine for his own use in 1908. The idea was taken up by his cousin, W. H. Hoover, and refined for manufacture. The Electric Suction Sweeper was soon in production. Its success in America was almost immediate, and the verb 'to hoover' entered the language. In Britain its progress was slower – electricity was not readily available in many households until after the First World War – but its ultimate success was inevitable.

Patricia's first egg

The evening was brightened, too, by a present from Patricia the chicken. Her first egg. 'It's beautiful brown,' said Ruth, 'and it's nice and speckly and it's lovely and warm and it's beautiful, I'm telling you. There was loads of squawking and things before, and we were like, "Oh what's going on?" Patricia came out and Dad checked and there was this beautiful egg. We ran up to Mum at the window and shouted, "Look, look, an egg!" And she came racing out, as did Kathryn and Joe.'

Paul, meanwhile, had been trying to finally sort out the continuingly frustrating range. 'It's not been producing what I want it to produce. I can see this fantastic glowing heat, producing gallons and gallons of heat but not gallons and gallons of hot water, so today I stripped it out completely, pulled it to pieces, cleaned it out and put it all back together again.'

He had found a 'significant block' between the grill and the heat exchanger: a lot of the old ash and burnt anthracite was clogging up the system and preventing the heat from getting to the exchanger. So now he had removed the ashtray. 'That's worked wonderfully well. So at last we've had hot water.' Finally, after a week of tepid strip washes, Paul had been able to have a bath; as had Joyce and Kathryn. And they had had wonderful jacket potatoes for supper, done in just a single hour. Fortified by this success, Joyce, too, was in a much better mood. 'I hope you enjoyed our Range Fancier's half hour there,' she chuckled at the video camera in the cupboard in their bedroom. 'And the next programme is beauty hints and tips from Joyce.' Over the last six days, she continued, she felt as if she'd put on sixty years' worth of wrinkles. The home-made face cream wasn't working, even when she warmed it up in warm water. 'But I now have some cold cream, which I could have bought in 1900 for 6d a jar and I feel much better.'

The house was cosy and dark. 'I feel all clean and lovely,' she said. The argument of the morning had receded. 'After we'd all shouted and cried and said, "Look, what are we doing here? What's all this for?" we realised we were enormously privileged and we've been more focused in what we're doing.' Now she felt the row was her fault. 'Because normally I'm the barometer of the family and people seem to kind of feed off me in a way. I can sense if somebody's a bit grumpy or on the brink. It's a sort of diplomacy thing. All mums do it. You know, you could get an award for it. Most mums are there kind of keeping everybody in balance. But today what happened was that I went off balance as well. I wasn't there as a constant. But I'm going to be much more positive in the morning. We're going to eat our porridge and see what tomorrow brings.'

Beside her in bed Paul was reading the 1900 edition of Cassell's *Encyclopaedia of Mechanics*. 'It's absolutely wonderful,' said Paul. 'You really could build a car chassis complete. It gives you all the dimensions and how to bend the wood and things like that. It just excites me to see things like that. Today it's all B&Q and Do-It-All , you just buy it off the shelf, and make it up from the leaflet.'

'Apparently,' commented Joyce, 'he thinks that by the end of three months he could have built me a car or something.' She was reading Hords *Comic Annual* of 1886. 'Paul's very serious, isn't he?' she wrote in her diary.

Sweets day

'Today is Saturday,' wrote Hilary in her diary. '*Sweets* day! Well, this morning I had the biggest lie-in I have ever had for ages! I woke up at about 7 a.m. when Joe did the chickens and came in my bed! Then I fell asleep until 9.30 a.m. when I woke up, emptied my potty, and changed.'

Paul had a less leisurely start. Going downstairs at 6.30 a.m., he found the range had gone out. After all the hard work of yesterday this might have depressed a lesser man, but not Paul. 'It's not a problem,' he told his video diary, 'it won't take me too long to light, and look, another surprise – egg number two.'

He thought it was Fortnum or Mason who had produced, rather than Patricia, because the shell was a different colour, indeed 'slightly cracked, with a bit of poo on it, but egg number two – very exciting. It really is wonderful. That's what I want to do every morning, when I get up and go down there – find an egg or two.' He had just caught sight of himself in the camera and he looked like 'the scruffiest devil in the universe'. 'So I'm going to have a lovely long shave,' he said.

Outside it was a fine spring morning. Standing at the window, Joyce was in fantasy mode. 'OK, so I'm a Victorian woman and I've been living here since 1892 – or perhaps we've just moved in, and I've brought all my precious belongings with me. My mangle, my copper, my crockery, my dishcloths, my clothes and I've moved into this lovely house and this morning, because the sun is shining, I thought I would do a little bit of hand washing.'

Above: *Joe feeding the chickens: Charlie, Patricia, Fortnum and Mason were a birthday present to his mother.*

A couple of hours later Victorian reality had caught up with her. 'I've just stood for nearly an hour washing up the dishes and cleaning the kitchen again because everything is covered in filthy muck and quite frankly I feel as if the joy has gone out of my life. I thought I'd do a bit of hand washing, so I got my washboard down, because the draining board is mucky and if you put anything there it gets dirty brown marks on it. I laid Paul's best things on the side, scrubbed them with the soap and the scrubbing brush, got the collars clean, thinking, "I'm really going now, I can see the end in sight, maybe another hour", and then I turn it over and the washboard is filthy. I'm bloody fuming! It looked fantastic, but as soon as it got wet and I put something on it, it covered everything in dirt. It's disgusting!

'I just think, this poor woman, who must have been chained to the kitchen, you can't even sit in the nice rooms, you can spend hours getting the nice rooms nice, but you can't sit in them, you can't enjoy them, because you are chained to the kitchen and the scullery. I wanted to time-travel, I really did, but it's such hard work. My hands are sore, my skin's all dry, it's not idyllic, it's not romantic, it's dirty, and maybe because I know there's an alternative, just feet away, across the fence, next door, it makes me feel all the worse. Maybe if I felt everybody was in the same boat, I would have accepted my lot, my station in life, just got on with it.

'If it weren't for Paul,' she continued, 'I mean I know I moan about him, oh God, Living By the Rules and all this stuff, but if it weren't for Paul getting up, and relighting the range and that sort of thing, I just don't know – I can't imagine a Victorian woman would have had a husband like the husband I've got. He's such a hard worker and he doesn't moan. It's me, really, I'm just not up to it.'

She decided to cheer herself up by washing her hair with a new preparation: egg yolk and lemon juice. And though it sounded improbable and disgusting, it was, with Paul's help, a success. 'It's really quite fluffy,' she enthused, when they'd finished, 'and not too bad, so thank God for little mercies. You wet your hair with lukewarm water, froth up the egg yolk and the lemon, rub it into your scalp, leave it for about a minute and then rinse it out with very, well, cool water, so you don't cook the egg, I suppose. I'm really, really pleased with the result, it's nothing like it was with the soap, which was awful, no matter how many times I rinsed it.'

> ## To keep butter in hot weather
>
> *In the absence of refrigerators it was a difficult business to keep items cool during hot weather. Although some grand establishments had ice-safes, most households had to rely on more ingenious methods:*
> *'It is a difficult matter to keep butter in warm water so as to send it to the table in a sweet, firm condition. To put the butter itself in water spoils it. The following is a simple and good method. Place the butter dish in a shallow vessel, such as a soup plate, in which cold water, mixed with common salt, has been put. Cover the dish, but not the vessel containing the water, with a flowerpot. Keep it in a cool place, in a draught if possible, and change the water often, and there will be no trouble with the butter.'*
> Madge's Book of Cookery

Fortified, Joyce was going to go back downstairs and get on with it. 'I really should try harder. I thought I was made of sterner stuff, but I'm just a weedy little 1999 woman who thinks she's bigger, braver and stronger than she really is. In actual fact I'm a pampered, lily-livered softy, who is learning a lot of lessons. I still want to get out into that sunshine. It seems wicked and cruel to have to spend the day stuck indoors, but maybe if I can crack on this morning, I can reward myself with something this afternoon. A turn around the park, or a trip to the Co-op to buy some toffees or something. Thank heaven for egg yolks! I actually used Fortnum's egg, because it was a bit cracked, so we thought we wouldn't eat it, but it made a fantastic hairwash – so thank you, Fortnum.'

Paul, meanwhile, besides washing his wife's hair and cleaning the house, had got the range going nicely again. It was the Coalite, he thought, that was just burning away and not holding the heat in, as coal would have done. But he had a little tip, from neighbour Kyungu (who had grown up with a range in the north country), which might prevent it from happening again. 'This is to use the coal dust from the bottom of the bunkers. Apparently we're supposed to wet that slightly and put it on top and that should keep the heat in.' By lunchtime they had moderately warm water in the pipes. 'I don't know that you'd call it warm,' Paul elaborated, 'but it's better than the cold stuff that comes out of the tap.' Whatever, he was happy. 'I am enjoying myself, I am continually working, but I am working for the house, for me, for my knowledge, and for Joyce and the children, to make sure their life is not fraught with disasters.' Joyce's egg-washed hair, he added, was beautiful. 'Well, I think it's beautiful, her hair would be beautiful anyway, whatever I washed it in, because she's beautiful.'

Lunch was 'only bread and jam', wrote Hilary. 'But at least none of it touched the RANGE!'

Below: A meal round the kitchen table. Joyce and Paul felt that Victorian routines brought the family closer together.

In the afternoon, leaving Kathryn alone in the house – 'with strict instructions to keep the chain on and not allow anybody to come in' – the rest of the family went for a walk to the shops. With washing and lunch out of

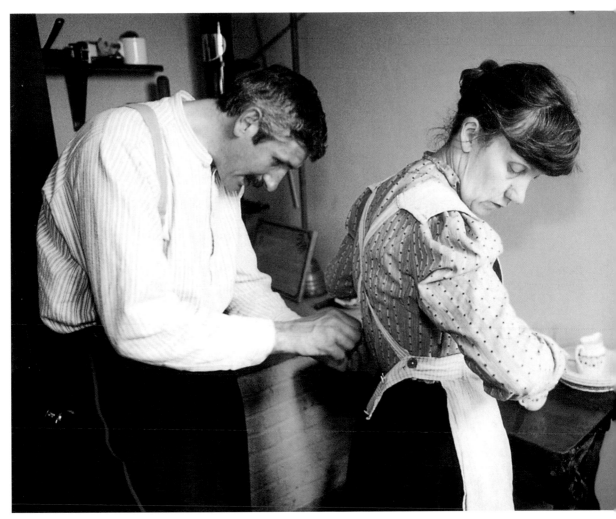

the way, and an evening meal of split pea and vegetable stew already prepared, Joyce had relaxed. 'The day is taking shape, it's quite nice.'

Up into Charlton they went in their Victorian clothes. 'We walked past two fish and chip shops,' said Joyce. But with Paul with them, they didn't succumb. They bought tea and writing paper and a selection of 1900 sweets. 'Everton mints and liquorice and sherbet lemons and some toffee, so the children can have a treat this afternoon for being so good.'

When they returned, the baker called. 'We went mad,' wrote Hilary, 'and bought nearly everything the baker had! We are mad on cakes now. We bought a Victoria sponge and then got given another cake from next door. We have so many visitors, I reckon they want to be on film.'

Above: *Paul does up Joyce's apron, which was, she said, 'a bit fiddly at the back'. Joyce wore the apron almost all the time when indoors, to protect her clothes against dust and ash. One of the great shocks of returning to 1900 was just how much dirt the house managed to generate, and how much extra work was required to clean it up. Joyce concluded that the Victorians would have become used to a lower level of cleanliness than today.*

Mrs. Newlywed. "AND TELL ME—WHAT IS MY POPSY'S LITTLE WIFE TO HIM?"
Mr. Newlywed (thinking of the bills). "OH—VERY, VERY *DEAR!*"

Above: *This* Punch *cartoon shows the man of the house dealing with the bills, but Paul and Joyce did this together in the 1900 House.*

Kathryn had meanwhile written, Ruth wrote, 'a 40-page 8-sided letter to her best friend Sharon'. She was not keeping a diary, nor being particularly forthcoming to the video diaries, sharing her troubles with Sharon instead. 'Kathryn looks very bored, believe me,' Ruth added.

Ruth had found a 'make your own theatre' among the toys. 'So,' said Hilary, 'we made our own.' It was a Victorian Pollock's theatre with cut-out cardboard actors from popular pantomimes. In the evening they put on a performance of *Cinderella*. Had the twins taken their inspiration from their mother? 'Oh dear, I spend all my time cooking and cleaning,' groaned their put-upon heroine.

Relaxing after his long day' the only thing Paul was missing was a wider contact with the outside world. 'We've been here a week and I haven't heard any news from anywhere, be it twentieth century or 1900. I've missed the *Daily Telegraph*, which I like to read on a Saturday. I'd like just a magazine, or something like that, to let me know what is going on in the world.

Joyce, however, had settled in with Cassell's *Book of the Household*. 'These books are fascinating!' she wrote in her diary. 'Paul and I keep reading bits out to each other and marvelling at them. He's been telling me about washing – especially washing of clothes by machinery. This got my hopes up, but all it meant was using a dolly tub thing. I've been reading about family life. The "master" or husband and father still has the say on everything in 1900. The only changes are in the Married Women's Property Acts of 1870 onwards. It's interesting to note that Cassell's saw these acts as working two ways. Firstly, to protect women, giving them some power and privilege. However secondly it placed "RESPONSIBILITIES UPON THEM OF WHICH BEFORE THEY KNEW NOTHING". Bloody cheek! *Still* assuming that women have neither the intelligence, the wit nor the ability to cope. Absolute rubbish! Men must have been scared witless. This must have been seen by many of them as the beginning of the end – the slippery slope. I've seen cartoons in another book depicting what a chaotic and hysterical place they thought Parliament would become if women were to be MPs – as if it weren't already. God, I feel so outraged inside I feel like standing for election myself! I've gone through the whole of women's struggle of the past century in one short week. We haven't come so far at all. Paul is great and I don't hate men

Above: *Watched by Ruth, Joyce works on the ledger. Their weekly budget was strictly set at a level appropriate to a warrant officer's earnings of the period. Joyce enjoyed the challenge of keeping within a budget, especially as it meant working in pounds, shillings and pence.*

at all, but I just bristle with righteous indignation when I see how women lived only a hundred years ago. Votes for women! We have a long way to go yet. We don't need to be "superior" *en masse* to men, but we need to be equal. OK, so I know I'm not saying anything new, but I've never felt so strongly about this subject before.'

Undressing that evening Joyce got a shock. 'My corset has kind of undone itself. I'm not the sylphlike thing I thought I was. It's the revenge of the cake. We've been going mad when the baker calls, because he arrives with lovely freshly baked bread, Eccles cakes, Bath buns and so on – I'm going to have to lay off cake for a bit, or else goodness knows what shape I'm going to be at the end of three months.'

A 1900 tea

In the morning Joyce sat down with her ledger and worked out for the first time what they had been spending and eating, and then planned a really healthy diet. Victorian vegetarians, she decided, would have eaten whatever was in season. 'Loads of fresh fruit and vegetables, and maybe fish one or two days a week. Milk, I've got down to two pints in the morning, two pints in the afternoon. The Co-op I'm going to use for odds and ends and I will avert my eyes when I pass by the shampoo. I love working in pounds, shillings and pence,' she added. 'Hate decimalisation. I can remember when I was sixteen and decimalisation arrived and I thought, "It's just horrible, really."'

Paul, meanwhile, was as busy as ever. 'I like getting to grips with the house,' he wrote in his diary. Up first, as always, he lit the dreaded range, which had gone out again. Then he cooked porridge for himself, Ruth and Joe. Then he waterproofed the henhouse he'd built ('just tacked on a bit of lino'). Then he attempted to 'modify' the copper ('but I'm afraid I may have broken it'). His prime concern was that both the family and the equipment were ready for their first wash day – tomorrow, Monday. Then he gave Joe a bath and cleaned out the bathroom.

'What a day!' he concluded. 'To top it all Joyce has cut her finger and I had to use the twentieth-century first-aid kit. She was messing around with a candle.'

That evening the family were invited for a relaxing Sunday tea over the road. Neighbours Fred and Ruth had laid on a thoroughly Victorian spread. Cucumber sandwiches, sausage rolls and scones. 'We didn't cheat,' said Paul. 'There were no Penguins, chocolate biscuits or anything like that on offer.' As they enjoyed this 1900 feast the family discussed their first week in the Victorian house. Joyce aired the problem of shampoo. Fred had a solution: Leave it alone. He himself hadn't washed his hair for seventeen years. 'I thought he was going to say seventeen days,' said Joyce later. 'Or seventeen months, but he said seventeen *years*. And his hair looked really nice. I know it's short, but he rinses it through with water and it cleans itself, he says. So from now on I'm not going to wash my hair. OK, if I start to attract various creatures to live in it, I may have to rethink, but I'm going to try, and see if it really does start cleaning itself.'

That evening Joyce was in a reflective mood, reconsidering the family's first week. 'Whenever I've read books about expeditions to the Antarctic or about people who have gone and climbed up Everest, they always seem to fall out with each other after about three days. And you think, "What on earth are they arguing for? They've only been living together a couple of days." And I've always thought, "what a bunch of precious, silly individuals." But in actual fact, it's very strange, when you're thrown out of your normal environment and you have a culture shock like this, even people like ourselves, who think we're a great team, even we seem to have fallen apart, so that every little thing that someone says or does, someone else will pick up on. I don't know, if they put the porridge in the wrong place or whatever, it just seems to be so important. All of a sudden what I've read about people going on expeditions together seems to make sense.

'But a good thing that has come out of it is we're finding out about each other in a way that could have taken us years, or maybe we'd never have found out about each other at all. It's wonderful for me to be able to see my children as complete human beings.

Above: *Ruth beats dust from the kitchen rag rug. The children helped with all the chores around the 1900 House.*

'I think now to make it work we've got to forget 1999, and all the things that we could have. I've got to forget thinking, "Oh this would be so much easier if I had detergent," or, "If I had my vacuum cleaner this would be so much cleaner." I've got to be more patient and accepting, try and keep optimistic, and calm down. I really do need to believe it's 1900. So I won't go to the Co-op very often, because there are too many temptations there.'

'I'm very optimistic about it all,' was Paul's first-week conclusion. 'I really want to do it, and I hope there is no such thing as failure. We're having to learn to order everything, just have a job for each day.'

A Pattern of Life

he family's first wash day was so exhausting that in the evening they were too drained even to talk to their video diaries. Joyce's Monday written diary read:

'Another entry by Ms Misery-guts.
Let's think positively.
1) The bed is very comfortable.
2) The copper heats up beautifully.
3) I love having black bits of coal up my nose.
4) I think I've got scurvy.
Goodnight, Joyce.'

But as the second week got under way, the Bowlers had begun to settle in properly. 'We're getting into a pattern of life for the 1900 House,' Paul reported. 'I get up at a quarter to six and there's no one up, so I can actually do breakfast. Make the porridge and toast and restoke the fire. Lay the table, make pots of tea, so it's all ready for when the others get up. Then that allows me, when they're downstairs just after seven, to go upstairs with the hot water I've now got and have a shave, tidy myself up for the day, and leave the house to catch my train at eight. When I come back at five, Joyce has been busy all day in the house and has in fact done everything. She cooks me a meal, I sit there, I volunteer to wash up, we sit down and have a quick chat about the day, a quick look at the accounts, see how we're getting on, then it's time for bed. I do feel as if the experience is levelling out.'

'This week has been calmer,' Joyce agreed, 'not so intense or hysterical. The feelings that were running through us last week, I don't know where they came from. It was the strangest thing – just bizarre. This week, thank goodness, it's slowed down, otherwise I think I would have gone stark staring mad.'

'This week's gone better than the last,' Hilary agreed, 'as I predicted. If every week's like this it's going to be a dream.'

Paul and Joyce's only worry was Joe, who didn't seem to be eating properly, refusing the

vegetarian meals Joyce was preparing and coming home from school with half his packed lunch still uneaten. 'He doesn't like any Victorian-style food,' Joyce complained. 'He's now talking about how he only wants to eat chicken

Above: *Ruth hangs her mother's drawers out on the line. After a couple of exhausting wash days, Joyce sent most of the family washing out.*

nuggets and cornflakes. He's being very stubborn.' 'I'm afraid,' said Paul, 'it's maybe going to have to be a concession that Joe eats something that he's used to eating outside of the house – some 1999 food.' Joe himself was clear what he wanted. 'Here's all the foods that I want,' he told the video diary. 'Peanut butter, chocolate spread, chips, cornflakes, ice cream, flip lollies, fruit pastilles, chocolate spread, spaghetti on toast, pasta, chicken drums and nuggets, and pizza.'

'Don't you like our Victorian cooking?' his mother asked him. 'No,' he replied.

The other worry was Paul's face, which after a week of cut-throat razor work looked, said

Laundry

No chore in the 1900 household was so exhausting and time-consuming as doing the washing. The pounding, rubbing, wringing and ironing of clothes, sheets and table linen was tiring work indeed. Any family that could afford it would send their washing out to be done professionally.

And it was in the commercial laundries that many of the technical innovations were first made that were later taken up and developed into domestic washing machines. Throughout the second half of the nineteenth century there were attempts to ease the lot of those washing at home. Mechanical devices were introduced which roughly replicated the actions of pounding the clothes with a 'dolly' or rubbing them on a wash board, but they tended to be as labour-intensive as the processes they were seeking to replace. The best machines of this type were the well-geared double-cylinder machines developed in the 1880s and 90s.

Further refinements saw the introduction of a gas-heating element to boil the water in the cylinder. In one model – the 'Factotum' – the heated cylinder, once drained, became converted into a rudimentary tumble-dryer.

It was, however, only with the application of the electric motor, in the years immediately after 1900, that these washing machines advanced significantly in effectiveness. The twin-tub machine evolved, which combined a washing and a spin-drying function. Even these machines were slow to enter domestic use. They became popular in America during the 1920s, but in Britain they were long considered an expensive luxury. They did not become readily affordable – and popular – until the end of the 1950s. In 1958, 29 per cent of families had a washing machine; one year later that number had risen to 64 per cent.

Ruth, 'as if he's been attacked by a cat'. 'I am getting better at it,' Paul observed, 'and slightly quicker, but I made a few mistakes in the beginning which are painful now because there are some nicks I've had, which get cut every time I have a shave. They're not healing properly.' He was worried about how he would appear in his new role at the Royal Marines Careers Centre in Kensington. 'I need to present myself in a correct way,' he said, 'if I'm going to meet the public in a public place.'

So it was decided he would pay another trip to Trumper's of Mayfair, for both a proper shave and a refresher course in technique. Paul was delighted. He took in his razor to show Gary the barber, and Gary showed him how to sharpen it correctly with a block and sharpening paste. 'I was cutting my face to bits because my blade wasn't sharp,' Paul realised. Gary loaded him up with Sandalwood and Rose shaving soaps and sent him off a happy man.

But when he returned home, he found that Joyce was up in arms with him about his day of luxury. Having left her hair unwashed for six days, she had finally felt so dirty and itchy she'd had a second attempt with raw egg and lemon. 'You will be thrilled to know,' she confided to her video diary, 'that it's still extremely sticky and disgusting. It worked once, but it doesn't work on six days' worth of grease and coal dust and whatever else I've got stuck in my hair.'

'As the female,' she elaborated, 'I have much more to put up with. As Paul is a man in the Royal Marines, you've basically got a chap who's given up hardly anything. He isn't really suffering, that's why it's easier for him. He's wearing clothes that aren't constricting him, or really strange at all. He's not wearing some weird contraption that means he can't go to the toilet without an enormous palaver. Then he started saying he didn't know how to shave and wasn't it sad, and oh dear, he cut his face – and he was whisked off to Trumper's in Mayfair. Where he's been given all sorts of things, beautiful lotions and potions to put on his face and enable him to have a smooth shave. I haven't been whisked off to a hairdresser's to enable me to learn how to wash my hair with possibly a natural product. No, it's been a baptism of fire for me. Soap and eggs. And then I was made to feel bad because I went and bought some shampoo and used it. Well, I'm sorry, but I think that whatever Paul has brought home from Trumper's today has some very strange ingredients that certainly weren't around in the year 1900. But then of course he's a man, isn't he? While I'm stood around with enough grease in my hair to fry a batch of chips. I don't mean to have a go at Paul, but it's the male thing, isn't it? Not just in 1900, but in 1999 I'm still the one that's coming off worse. It sounds like I'm jealous and, yes, I am jealous. Because he's a man and whether it's 1900 or 1999 he gets the better deal. Though I get the frillier drawers.'

Ironically, Paul was also confessing to jealousy. 'This is all developing into a wonderful experience,' he told his video diary, 'but I wish I could spend some more time at home and have that input that I think Joyce is having. I leave first thing in the morning and then when I come back in the evening the majority of the work is done, and all I get is the washing up and a few other bits to do.'

Wolf whistles and cars beeping

The family were now starting to meet people from the neighbourhood. Not just Ruth and Fred, and Kyungu, from across the road, but Lynn and Nick who lived next door but one, someone Joyce had met in the doctor's surgery, and so on. 'So that's nice for Joyce,' Paul said, 'and they're all very interested in what we're doing and some of them have got a good outline of why we're here.'

'Lots of people are saying hello to me now,' said Joyce, 'and I'm smiling at everybody in the hope that they will respond. I'm getting some response back and it's lovely. I think they understand it's difficult for us. I haven't had anybody come up to us and say, "Oh I wish I was doing what you're doing, I bet it's a doddle." Most people say, "Oh, I couldn't do that. Couldn't give up my washing machine."' Two people in the street had even offered Joyce the use of their automatics. 'I know what it's like, dear,' they'd told her. 'You know it won't be any trouble just to run a load through.' 'And it's extremely kind of them,' Joyce said, 'and I'm very, very tempted, but they don't seem to understand that the purpose of the exercise is for us to see if we can survive under 1900 conditions.'

A day or two later she added, 'They've made cakes, they've invited me round for cups of tea, and it's very

Social etiquette

There was, throughout the late-Victorian period, an elaborate etiquette of visiting observed by all people with pretensions to respectability. There were strict rules as to whom one could visit and how one should call upon them. The practice of paying calls and leaving cards was particularly the preserve of women; it was one of the ways they could fill their days while their husbands – and their servants – were at work. Except in the case of relatives, women could only call on other women, and even then only after an initial introduction had been effected by a third (and already known) party.

There were strict rules for paying visits. Many women had recognised 'At Home' days on which they would receive callers, generally between the hours of three and six; it was, of course, best to pay one's visit on this appointed day.

There were numbers of social commentators eager to give advice on how to proceed. The woman of 1900 was advised to put on her prettiest gown, and arm herself with her calling cards and 'a liberal supply of small talk'. On calling at the house of her acquaintance or friend she should not send up her card (a coarse 'business custom') but instead enquire of the servant (who would be sure to open the door) whether the mistress of the house was at home. On receiving the answer 'yes', follow the servant to the drawing-room door. Give her your name, pronouncing it clearly. She will then announce you. Enter the room 'gracefully and composedly' (an art which the novice visitor is advised to study). Shake hands with your hostess.

You might be shown to a seat, but were unlikely to be introduced to all the other guests present. On sitting down it was your duty to make conversation with those around you. Commentators advised against 'servants' or 'domestic matters' as topics of conversation. At some point during the call it is likely that tea will be offered. 'Five o'clock tea' was something of a Victorian invention. Previous generations would have offered wine and cake to callers. A call should last about fifteen minutes, and never over half an hour. These times, however, had to be judged; one must never look at one's watch.

Having risen to depart, 'you must not keep your hostess standing a long time talking while you say your adieus'. Your hostess will say goodbye to you at the drawing-room door. When leaving the house, place your card on the table in the hall, also your husband's card. On subsequent visits you need only place your husband's card.

If, for any reason, the person on whom you were calling was 'not at home', you should leave your card. And if you wished to terminate an acquaintance you might call and leave a card without enquiring whether your host or hostess were at home or not.

odd really, because I'm sure if we'd just bought this house and moved in as the Bowler family, 1999, I'd probably never have met any of these people. But there's a novelty to us, and I think everybody's feeling a bit sorry for us, seeing us wandering around in these clothes and probably wondering what it's like inside. But in actual fact we're doing them a service because we've got everybody talking to each other.

'I didn't realise,' she continued, 'how much I would miss going to work outside of the home and little things in the morning like being able to talk to people. I mean I popped into the school office this morning to get the term-time dates for Joe and had a bit of a chat – and it was like a shot in the arm. Just to be able to get out of the house and talk to people. And I think that would have kept the 1900 lady sane. You would have been desperate for some social contact and I'm sure people were in and out of their houses a lot more than they are now. Everyone seems to keep themselves to themselves these days.

'I was reading this free paper that was shoved through the door last night. We ummed and aahed as to whether we should read it because it wasn't a 1900 newspaper, but I just needed to read this newspaper and I thought, "It's not cheating, someone shoved it through the door." So I read it from cover to cover, all the small ads as well and now I know everything about Charlton and Woolwich – even the name of the local MP. And there was a whole section of Lonely Hearts, I suppose you'd call it. Women looking for men and men looking for women and all that stuff. There was a little column at the end where people were just looking for friends. No sexual contacts, nothing like that. They simply wanted some friends to go and have fun with, a cup of tea with, to share a bottle of wine with, go shopping with – they simply want friends. Now it could be that they've moved around the country and they're new to London. But I don't think that's always the case. It's just a shame that in today's society we all shut ourselves off from each other. Maybe things like radio and TV have made that easier, because we think we're having social contact because we see the newsreader every day, or the presenter of a programme every day. But they don't know us and we don't know them. It's very strange.'

Hair washing

There was much debate around 1900 on the subject of hair washing, and the frequency with which it should be attempted. Some authorities complained that hair became 'uncomfortably dry and brittle... and unmanageable' if washed too often. Others suggested that 'the brisk rubbing with a coarse towel after shampooing is of immense advantage in stimulating and promoting the growth of hair'. The common practice of washing the hair in cold water with the intention of strengthening it was condemned by 'Isobel', the editor of Pearson's Home Management, *as having the opposite effect: 'it will make the hair thin, turn grey and become dull'.*

There remained, however, a general distrust of wetting the hair too much. Cassell's guide went so far as to suggest that the hair could be kept clean merely by rubbing 'a decoction of rosemary over the head with a sponge'. Edward Spon in his Household Manual *was less hydrophobic; he recommended 'a good shampoo every week or ten days for those persons exposed to a good deal of dust, and every two to three weeks for other people' as being 'sufficient for cleanliness'.*

The 'shampoo' to be employed in these operations bore little resemblance to what we use today. It had to be made up at home. Common late-Victorian shampoo recipes included soap and water, borax and water, egg yolk beaten with lime water, egg yolk beaten with 'a little subcarbonate of potash' and ammonia dissolved in soapy water. This last recipe was recommended as being particularly good for blondes, as it produced a beautiful auburn tint. Ready-made shampoo mixtures were only just beginning to be introduced in 1900. They originated in Paris and, as a result, were regarded as being more than a little risqué.

Most of the neighbours had been friendly, but one day this one short lady with greyish hair had come up to Joyce when she was out with Kathryn and the twins and said, 'Are you doing a re-enactment?' 'And the girls,' Joyce explained, 'were feeling quite self-conscious, so I just said, "No, these are our clothes, we wear them."' The lady had walked off and Joyce had thought nothing more of it – until a couple of days later when she accosted Joyce again. 'I'd just like to say you were very rude to me and very hostile,' this lady had told her. 'Well, I'm sorry,' Joyce had replied. But the lady was upset. 'She'd really got herself into a bit of a state, and she stalked off, very, very angry. I'm sorry if she thought I was rude, but I wasn't rude. And I was thinking about it on the way back, and it upset me, because I thought, it was wrong that people could think, just because you're dressed differently, they've got a right to come up and have a go at you. Of course we're going to attract some attention. I've had wolf whistles and cars beeping and people shouting, "Ooh er, Missus, what are you dressed as?" But she seemed to think she deserved a full-blown explanation of my life.'

Paul had adopted another way of dealing with people who came up and asked him what he was doing in period costume. 'I just say, "I'm a time-traveller, and I've travelled back to 1900 with my family and we are living in a beautiful, restored house in Charlton." So I don't have to go into the whys and wherefores of what we're doing.'

Putting up with it

In the middle of this second week Joyce was cheered up by a visit from her eldest daughter Connie. 'Her initial reaction to the house has been very interesting,' she reported. 'She thought it smelt of gas, and she just can't believe how we're living the way we are. To see her Mum with her hair like this, sitting by candlelight and so on – I think she's quite impressed. But she can't stay more than two nights and maybe I don't blame her. I think if I was nineteen, and I had a hot shower and a job elsewhere to go to, I might find that more attractive.'

The family celebrated the eldest's arrival with a special meal – fish and chips – as they had discovered there would have been fried-fish shops in 1900. 'Which was lovely,' said Ruth. 'It was cod, I think. Anyway, a really, really nice piece of fish and lots of chips as well.'

Connie wore a corset for a morning before taking it off. 'She just couldn't stand it,' said Joyce. 'Connie is just so normal,' Ruth commented the next day. 'She can't wear a corset, so all today she just wore her dress. And it was strange because she just looked a funny shape.'

Connie was company for Joyce as she cleaned the house. Then at midday, they sat down with the Victorian manuals and tried to find another way of washing Joyce's hair, which was 'still greasy and full of egg'. 'Then we thought, rosemary, the herb rosemary is very good for your hair. So we made an infusion with hot water and some sprigs of rosemary which a kind neighbour gave me, and rinsed and rinsed and now, this is the end result. It doesn't feel great, obviously it hasn't had conditioner on it, but it feels less greasy.'

The second week passed. Connie returned home. Joyce decided to send her laundry out, which she had read was entirely authentic, and cost her 2/- a load. 'I just want to say how thrilled I am with the laundry service,' she announced when the clothes and sheets returned. 'They're obviously extremely efficient. Sheets aren't over-starched. Clothes aren't over-blued.'

At the weekend Joyce's childhood friend Natalie came to call, bringing a basket of fruit and vegetables authentic to the period – another great treat for Joyce. Paul, meanwhile, was

contemplating growing a moustache. 'I think I might give it a go, for the simple reason that I keep cutting my top lip shaving. It might also look more in keeping with the part, like a lot of photographs that I've seen.'

Hilary had been given some watercolours and an easel to keep her busy, and Ruth a doll, which she named Adele and took everywhere. Joe was enjoying looking after the chickens and playing with his soldiers. A compromise had been reached on his desire for modern food. He was eating lunch at school, but sticking to the family's 1900 diet in the evening.

Only Kathryn was unhappy. She was thoroughly bored with the whole experience. 'I was thinking there is no point in being here, because all the focus is around Mum and Dad. I wanted to come and do the Victorian project because I thought it would be an adventure. I'm not saying I thought it would be a doddle, or not hard work, but I thought it would be stepping back in time, seeing how my ancestors would have lived, a fantastic and unique experience.

Opposite: *Hilary painting a watercolour of 50 Elliscombe Road. Painting was an enthusiasm she brought with her to the 1900 House.*

Above: *Hilary's watercolour portrait of Ruth and her doll on the bed the twins slept in together. Kathryn shared the small room too.*

I'm not denying that it is, but and this is a big BUT, I've experienced it for two weeks now and I'm sick of it. At home, I go out at least once a week, and even if it's just a video and pizza evening, or eating loads of chocolate ice cream round at my friend Sharon's house, it will make me happy. I'll be in a good mood for the rest of the week. We always have things lined up and plan things for the future, like we might go to a concert, or it'll be somebody's birthday party – and here I don't do anything at all. To be honest, I don't particularly want to know what a Victorian girl of my age would want to do, because all I've seen is embroidery, or playing the piano, or helping Mum out cleaning.'

She was going to bed with the others at about eight o'clock. 'I don't feel like I'm doing anything, except I'm really tired and the house is depressing me a lot.' She was sharing a room with her sisters, and there was nothing there that was hers. 'None of it is mine to do what I want to do with it. At home I've got all my knick-knackery and my books and my bed and

Opposite: *Ruth with her doll Adele. Ruth took the toy with her everywhere and even copied Adele's Victorian hairstyle.*

Above: *Kathryn at the piano. She took three lessons with a professional, but was not inspired to continue. The music she missed was contemporary 'house' and 'garage'.*

it's all mine. Here, not even the bed is mine. The pictures on the walls, I didn't choose them, I don't even know where they come from, and it just depresses me to think I'll be stuck in this house for another three months.'

As for the house itself, the range was still giving the family trouble. Some days it was working and others it was giving them no joy. 'We feed that furnace twenty-four hours a day,' Paul reported, 'and it's kicking out some heat, but the hot water situation is, it will give us between two and three inches of warm water for a bath, and then it goes cold and you have to start all over again.' The oven section just wasn't hot enough to be useful. Paul had tried to bake a cake, which had been 'a miserable failure'. Then they had left some baked potatoes in for fourteen hours and they were still 'as hard as rock'. Joyce felt that without the use of the oven the meals she was preparing were becoming repetitive.

Cleaning was still, Joyce found, a struggle. 'Paul keeps saying, "Oh, you're doing all this hard work," but I'm not. The only rooms I'm working on are the kitchen and the scullery, concentrating on the things that are keeping us surviving. Somebody suggested we do spring cleaning, well – expletive deleted – just living here, it feels like spring cleaning every day.'

Now, by the end of week two, they had learnt to accept, she reckoned, a new idea of what was clean. 'Because I don't have any electrical things to suck up the dust and every time I wipe something my cloth gets so dirty I want to wash it, I think we're living with a level of dirt and putting up with it. I can't disinfect things, I can't wipe surfaces clean with my antibacterial sprays and things, nothing ever looks sparkling, the sink has always got a bit of scum in it – you just have to accept it otherwise you don't get to bed at night. I've never been in a house that could generate so much dirt.'

Opposite: *Joyce laces Kathryn into her corset. Both mother and daughter came to feel that this restrictive garment was changing their physical shape.*

Even doing what she saw as the minimum Joyce was, she complained, 'knackered'. Part of it was that she was doing all the work in her corset. Paul had now been given a pair of moleskin trousers for house and garden tasks, and Joyce was envious. 'I would love to be able to get up in the morning, have my hair down, put on Paul's rough trousers, perhaps hold them together with a belt round the middle if they're too baggy, then one of his shirts, and spend the day like that, but I feel I'd be betraying what we're supposed to be doing. I think the whole thing would fall to bits.

'It's not just the tight waist,' she went on, 'it's the fact that from here down to here you are cased in body armour. It'd be fine if I was Lady Muck and I was going out to tea with somebody and possibly writing a few letters, interviewing the maid or the cook. But the fact is I'm not, so I take my hat off to these women who must have worn corsets and worked in them.' Though Joyce reckoned they wouldn't have worn them all the time. 'I don't think they were stupid. I think they only put it on maybe when they went out. If they were going to do the washing or whatever, they wouldn't have worn it.'

Paul, meanwhile, though he could hardly bear to admit it, was getting rather bored at work. 'I haven't got a key role when I get there,' he confided to his video diary. And being in central London he was surrounded with 1999 temptation. Sent over the road one morning to buy milk and doughnuts for the other workers in the Royal Marines Careers Centre, he found it hard

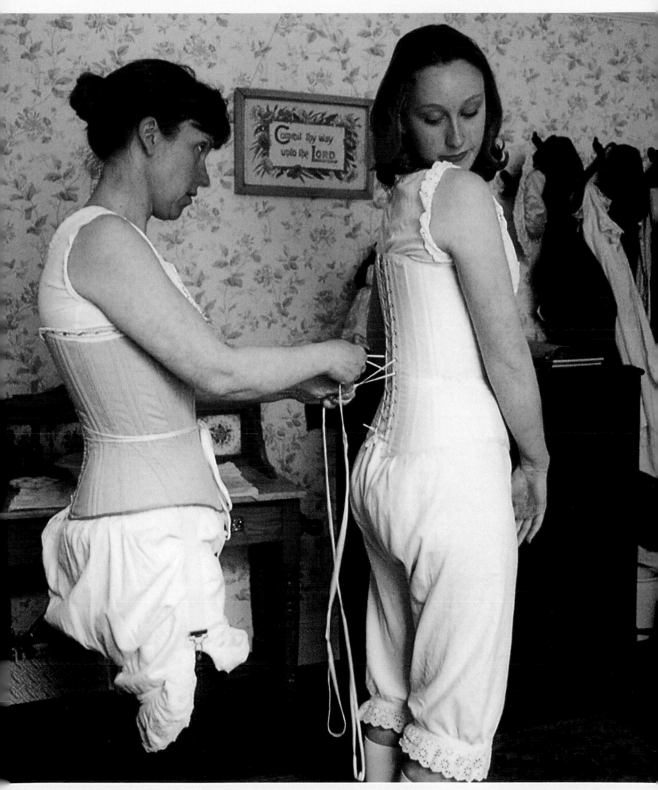

Above: *An extract from Cassell's 1900* Book of the Household *advises the Victorian father on his duties.* 'I'd like to rip that page out,' said Paul.

walking round Safeways, with all the modern luxuries and foods packing the aisles around him. 'I got a receipt for the exact amount, and then I went back there and made sure the person who gave me the money saw the change, just in case anybody made a comment. I want to stick to 1900 and I am sticking to it.'

But he didn't want to become the kind of 'master of the house' portrayed in Cassell's *Book of the Household*.

'He is the chief, the most indispensable member thereof. He holds the place of highest honour; he is the supporter and sustainer of the establishment. Should difference of opinion arise amongst the members of the family, he is the determining authority; he decides what is best to be done, and his decision carries weight. He stands in the thick of the fight; he bears the brunt of the conflict; and protects those whom he loves from danger and from harm.'

'I'd like to rip that page out,' Paul said.

Period drama

Now, as the third week in the house began, the clocks went back, and the longer, lighter evenings gave the family another hour before the candles had to be lit. Kathryn's mood had at last improved, after her first day at her new Saturday job, working in costume at Charlie the greengrocer's up the road, which was 'brilliant', and very different from her Safeways Saturday job at home.

Sitting in the garden reading with a cup of tea, Joyce had dropped off to sleep and been woken by 'this most fantastic sound'. 'It was a mixture of Latin American and jazzy saxophone music. I thought it was coming from next door, and it sounded like it was getting a bit quieter, so I walked right up to the fence and listened. I'd forgotten how much I miss music, but it was a really fantastic bit of music and then it came to an end and I could hear this little bit of conversation and now they'd put on something else, and I couldn't hear it, it wasn't loud enough, and I felt like shouting over the fence, "Can you turn that up, please?" Normally when you've got neighbours playing music you feel like saying, "Can you turn that off, please?" And I realised how much I missed modern music. It made me feel quite emotional, because I don't play the piano and

I'm not musical, but I miss it terribly. I want to go back in the garden now and see if they might play something else. There's a little spot in the garden where you can dance a bit and nobody can see you.'

Above: *After a few weeks, Kathryn got a Saturday job with Charlie Judd, a local greengrocer. Victorian children often started working at a young age.*

Another night Joyce had popped round next door to return a plate that had come with a cake her neighbour had given the family. 'And I went into the kitchen and she had lots of lights on, spotlights and things, and it really hurt my eyes, going from our house, which is very gloomy, with candlelight and gaslight. I kept saying, "Isn't it bright in here." I was thinking, "Why has she got all these lights on, you don't really need them." So obviously I've got attuned to the darkness and gloom in our house, and us going to bed at eight o'clock and so forth. We were just going to bed and she was just beginning to cook supper – she had a young friend round. While I can't contemplate doing anything after eight o'clock because it feels like three in the morning.'

Now, two weeks earlier than expected, Joyce got her period. 'And yes, I am making my own sanitary towels and I will be soaking them in the bucket, but I'm not going to soak them

Above: *Kathryn's job was a welcome break from Victorian routines and restrictions. She continued, however, to wear her 1900 clothes under her overalls.*

in salt water because as far as I can make out soda crystals were just as cheap as salt, and they're more effective, I think. In due course I will be washing the blasted things and we'll see how it goes. I must admit I've been out this morning and I was extremely wary as to whether I would come back in a bit of a mess.' But the towels she had made were double thickness compared to the ones she'd been shown at Shugborough, so she thought they'd be more effective. Perhaps, she mused, this was why she had been feeling so edgy and aggressive all the previous week. 'Why I felt like becoming the Charlton Strangler.'

Joyce and Paul had been talking quite a bit about the differences between 1999 and 1900; and how 1999 people, as they saw it, sentimentalised 1900. 'We've been talking about how some people are very keen to adopt Victoriana in their lives. They get the brass bed, or the old-fashioned bath, and think, "Isn't this twee, isn't this lovely, we could live like this." But what they don't realise is that they've sanitised Victoriana and made it into a 1999 version. You've

I am putting the coal in the cooker.

Above: *Another of Joe's drawings of life in the 1900 House. The range was central to the Bowlers lives and was to prove to be one of the more difficult things for the family to get used to.*

still got your central heating boiler, your washing machine, your power shower, but you kid yourself that you're living this almost Victorian life, when you're not. All this may look lovely, but when you start living in it, you realise how impractical a lot of it was – I mean, most of these ornaments and stuff are just dust collectors.'

Though they were living the 1900 experience properly, the time had now come for a little 1999 help – with the recalcitrant range, which had been nothing but trouble from the start of the time-travel experiment. Early on the Tuesday morning heating engineer Mike Bishop and his team arrived to fix this crucial piece of machinery. 'It will all be finished by the time I get home from school,' said Hilary, 'so that will be good. So I won't have to see it being ripped out, because I love the little range. I think it's doing as hard as it can, it's trying it's best and it's not its fault that it can't do it. It's a hundred years old and it can't do what a two-year-old cooker would do.'

The team took the range out, removed the back plate, brought the heat exchanger forward and produced so much dust that first Joyce, and then Paul, who had stayed behind from work specially to help in any way he could, left the house and went up onto Blackheath for a walk. 'It was just awful,' Paul confided later to his video diary, 'because they are from 1999 and they just came in and spoilt everything for me.' The builders with their mobile phones and bottles of Coke and twentieth-century language had turned the place back, Paul felt, into a 'restoration project' – rather than their 1900 House. 'It was like we were back at square one, day one.' But by the following afternoon the range was finally fixed, and producing proper hot water at last.

'I have had a fantastic bath,' Joyce reported that evening. 'Feel like I've died and gone to heaven. Hot water, soap, good scrub all over and I've sent out for some borax and camphor, so that I can try out my latest shampoo recipe.' It now took just two or three hours to heat up a bath's worth, rather than the best part of a day. The oven was working properly and boiling the kettle took just eighteen minutes, which was, as Joyce said, 'much better than the two and a half hours of before'. She baked a cake which took just two hours. 'Which has knocked off twelve hours from the previous record,' Paul wrote in his diary. 'Mike's done a fantastic job.'

'Things have been looking up,' said Hilary. 'Everything is sorting itself out.' Only Kathryn demurred. 'I'd just like to say that I'm trapped in this godforsaken dump and I bloody hate it here and I want to go home,' she told her video diary.

The daily tub

The Victorian dictum that 'cleanliness is next to godliness' still held some force in 1900. Bathing was both a sanitary and a moral imperative. The abiding – and peculiarly British – bathing tradition revolved around 'the daily tub', a cold bath taken first thing each morning. For the best effects the bath should be followed by 'much friction with a rough towel'. The combination of cold water and hard rubbing was regarded as 'an excellent invigorator and nerve bracer'.

In the mid-Victorian period, before plumbed-in bathrooms became common, the cold bath was generally accomplished with a sponge, a vessel of cold water, and a free-standing tub. But, by 1900, the plunge into the bathtub ready-filled with cold water was more general. Nevertheless there were signs that this stern regime was beginning to be modified. Cold baths came to be considered as suitable only for the robust. Those of a nervous disposition, it was said, were not to attempt them. Pearson's household guide affirmed that 'it is safe to say that no girls between the ages of thirteen and sixteen should be permitted to take absolutely cold baths'. Some doctors recommended tepid or even moderately warm water for the morning bathe. Other authorities, however, went further. There were those who proclaimed the benefits of the hot bath. They made no claims for its invigorating qualities, but suggested it was better for sanitary, cleansing and 'beautifying' purposes. 'A toilet or beautifying bath should be about the temperature of 70° to 75° Faht. and may be taken day and day about with a cold one, if the latter is permitted.'

Extra care, however, had to be taken of the face; it must not be washed too often. As one pundit remarked, 'Many skins will not stand constant washing, a practice which indeed tends to coarsen the complexion.' One wash a day was the maximum permitted. Showers were uncommon. Some firms produced elaborate spray apparatuses, but these were regarded either as luxurious curiosities or medical aids.

Historical tableau on legs

On Maundy Thursday Hilary had a confession to make. 'Today at school my friend gave out Cadbury's Creme Eggs to the whole class and I had one, so I've been very naughty. I like Creme Eggs though, they're gorgeous. But we can't have them any more because we're doing this. So when we go back home I'm going to buy all the cheap ones, because after Easter they're all cheap, so you grab them, you have about ten or fifteen in your basket and it's like £2.50 for all of them.' Her father had no idea of her wicked behaviour. In his diary Paul wrote, 'No choc eggs this year. The girls and Joe will be very disappointed. The year 1900 can be very disappointing.'

Meanwhile, the weather had turned warm and springlike. 'The rest of the world, it seems,' Paul wrote, 'has gone into sleeveless shirts, shorts, sandals and sunglasses. Oh how I wish I could do that. I am hot. My jacket seems so restrictive and I want to take it off, but I can't because I want to stay true to 1900.' The warmer temperatures had affected Hilary too. 'Everybody keeps asking me, "Are you cold? You must be freezing with no central heating." But it's not cold at all, it's boiling. I am boiling just in my nightie in the night. With this many clothes we don't need central heating.'

On Good Friday Joyce saw a man jogging past the front door in T-shirt and shorts. 'It's lovely weather,' she said. 'Needless to say Paul and I want to go for a run. But what can we wear?' Quite apart from wanting the exercise, she was starting to get worried about her appearance. 'I think I am changing shape,' she told her video diary. 'I am getting an enormous backside and belly and I seem to be going in at the waist. I don't know if I'm imagining this but I took a look at myself in the full-length mirror and it was not a pretty sight. I think I am putting on weight. Could there be a redistribution of fat at this stage?'

Instead of a run Joyce and Paul decided to take the family out to the Maritime Museum at Greenwich. 'I think it's going to be a bit boring,' said Hilary 'because it's Mum and Dad's decision where we go, so it's going to be awful. I mean, no offence to Mum and Dad, but – ships – they are the most boring subject to read about. Ugh! Anyway, I'm going to try and enjoy this holiday as much as I can.'

But as it turned out it was an excursion all except Kathryn enjoyed thoroughly. 'We went to the *Cutty Sark*,' Hilary reported that evening, 'which was excellent. The boat is massive and you get to see under the ground and in the ship and everywhere.

'It was wondrous,' Joyce said, 'to see how far ladies' fashion moved from the year 1900 until the 1920s. It really hit home today when I was walking round the Maritime Museum and you could see how in just twenty to thirty years the acceptable shape of women had changed completely. I just looked so longingly at the poster, I couldn't believe it was only 1928 – only twenty-eight years from now. I obviously then would have been seventy – oh God I'd have been in my seventies, but to think that women were freed from all this corsetry and had labour-saving things too. Possibly the older ladies thought it was shocking. These young things who cut their hair and didn't have waists. But the woman on the 1920s poster looked so free. I'm going to get hold of a copy and have it framed and put it on the wall at home. She's reclining there on a deckchair in a beautiful sleeveless shirt, with a beautiful pair of silk stockings and a pair of comfy shoes. After another eleven-hour-day in a corset she just looked like a dream to me.'

The only drawback was the attention they attracted in their Victorian clothes. 'It was really hard,' said Hilary, 'because everybody kept going, "Why are you dressed like that? Are you showing off? What's this in aid of?" And I was just going, "Oh, we're doing a documentary for Channel 4 and we have to wear this." It was so annoying. Kathryn was in a real mood.'

'I didn't really enjoy being the main attraction,' Joyce confessed. 'While lots of people thought we were working, either at the *Cutty Sark* or the museum, it kind of spoiled the day – I know it did for Kathryn. People are so well meaning and curious, of course they are, I would be exactly the same, and I don't mind that. But it's the fact that you look as if you're showing off and you're not. I mean, if we were out there going "Look at me! Look at me! Don't I look like the dog's wotsits?!" that would be different – but we were just trying to have a nice day out. So we've decided to stay at home tomorrow, not exactly to lick our wounds, but recover from what was a bit of an ordeal really.'

So on Easter Saturday, a little chastened, the Bowlers stayed at home. The weather wasn't good, it was no real temptation to go out. Paul was missing his weekend newspaper. 'I would love a *Daily Telegraph*, so I can pore over it all day, picking it up, reading the travel, looking at the magazine, drinking tea and just relaxing.' The man next door had gone away for the holiday and left the family a box of vegetables and a copy of the *Guardian* to read. 'Are they trying to tempt us?' Joyce asked. 'Are they trying to sabotage what we're trying to do?'

Later Nanny Bowler came to call on the family, with Joyce's sister Katrina and brother Toby. 'It was so great to see them,' Joyce wrote in her diary. 'We drank loads of tea and they ate all our digestive biscuits. At 1/4d a packet they were for Special Visitors only.' They brought with them welcome news. Nanny Bowler had found out in a newspaper article that the Victorians would have had Easter eggs and had brought some with her. The children were delighted. 'I'm so glad,' said Ruth, 'because we've got chocolate Easter eggs and I've eaten all of mine because I'm naughty.'

Easter Sunday was another beautiful sunny day. 'It's the sort of day,' said Joyce, 'when you just want to get up and get out. But I'm a bit hesitant, because of what happened on Friday. I felt like a walking attraction, this historical tableau on legs.' Once again she was fantasising about getting athletic. 'With this cakes and bread bonanza we've been having, I just feel so heavy. I feel like an enormous lardy lump and I'm sure I've put on weight. I have this horrible saggy backside and this enormous belly. I need to be able to do some physical exercise, which also stops me from feeling a bit down. It would be wonderful to go for a run this morning. I suppose I could put together something with Paul's underwear or mine or something, but then I would have to run in my boots, so I don't know, I'd probably get shin splints or blisters or something.'

In the end, despite their experience of Friday, Joyce girded up her loins and got everyone together and off the family went to the Horniman Museum in Forest Hill. They loved the exhibition, and Joyce felt she was enjoying the stuffed birds and tropical fish all the more because she was seeing them through unstimulated Victorian eyes.

But then, once again, they found themselves attracting attention, some of it of an unpleasantly 1999 variety. Waiting for the train on Forest Hill station they were accosted by a group of people whom Joyce described first as travellers. 'But they weren't really bona fide travellers. They were just people dressed in, you know, Doc Marten's boots, without laces, and an assortment of upper garments, facial piercing, wild hair, drinking cider and Tennants or whatever, and they starting effing this and effing that and one of them said, "I wonder what they're effing up to?" Pointing at us, so we just stood there very quietly. Then another of them said, "Are you the effing Railway Children?" And they started chattering among themselves. Then he said, "I expect they're looking at us and thinking we're funny. I expect they think we're dressed funny. I bet they do." And they were really speaking so loudly, it was like they were trying to elicit a response and the only response I wanted to give them really was just to turn round and say, "I don't mind how you dress, I'm not going to lower myself or be unkind to you by shouting a comment about how you dress on a station, in front of all the other people, in their hearing." It was just depressing, because they themselves weren't conforming to normal standards, dressing in a socially acceptable way, and yet they still had the gall to start talking about the way we were dressed, abusing us and trying to get us to respond. I couldn't believe they would be so unkind and bigoted.'

It hadn't been much better on the crowded Easter Day train. 'I'm finding London a difficult place to be in,' Joyce continued. 'We tried to shut our eyes and ears, but we had to travel on this train to get to the Museum and back, and it was filthy, full of people effing and blinding. I had to just rise above it and ask the children to ignore the swearing and showing off. I mean there were young children on that train – where their parents thought they were I have no idea – running up and down swearing and shouting at people, calling us names, and we had to just sit there and take it, because we're polite and civilised and kind. And I could see Paul sometimes just gritting his teeth and clenching his fists because he felt so powerless and vulnerable, because he wanted to stop them from doing it, but you can't, that is obviously the way society is here.

'I feel ashamed. People must be coming from all around the world to London and this is what they see. They see filth, they see people who don't care, money being poured into something like the Millennium Dome and the basic fabric of society is so threadbare you can see through it.

'It's another world. I'm not streetwise and I'm not hard, I'm friendly, I'll talk to people. I mean, a crowd of kids on the way to the station shouted, "What are you doing that for?" and I said, "Oh we're making a programme for the television" and one of them came up and he sort of touched me, it was almost a punch, he looked into my eyes; I saw conflict, hostility, aggression and I probably looked back with confusion, not fear, and then they don't know what to do because they haven't got the response they want, so they start swearing at you.

'So I'm afraid I'm finding the whole going out thing a real trial after that. I can just about get to Blackheath, or to the Co-op and back, before I start feeling scared. Yes, I think I'm scared.'

The Servant Problem

After their experiences in the outside world of 1999, on Easter Monday the family decided to remain in their 1900 haven. In her diary that evening Joyce wrote: 'As Kathryn said earlier, eloquently I thought, "You get bloody stared at when you go out and it's like a prison indoors." Ah, happy days. We are all going a little stir crazy. Kathryn is notching the days off on a chair leg. Ruth is talking to herself. Paul and Joe are re-enacting Waterloo (or is it the World Cup?) with Joe's soldiers in the garden and Hilary is in the bath scrubbing soot out of her nasal passages. Due to the entire family going down with sugar deprivation we felt the need to overdose on 2lbs of Victorian-style pick 'n' mix. Now we feel a bit sick, but it was worth two bob (2/- to you).

'Now I am feeling very literary,' she continued, 'as I sit reading in the gloom of late afternoon – coming down from my sugar rush. I may turn to the Gees linctus to see me through the night. How I wish I could pretend to enjoy a small volume of Byron or Hood to while away the hours, when in reality I'd rather have a half hour of Harry Hill.'

> The members of a family in the habit of going annually to the seaside for health and pleasure should all—*mater* perhaps excepted—take swimming exercises; the enjoyment in bathing is then very much enhanced. Instead of the somewhat vulgar pastime of paddling, the children can then take a swim; using caution, however, and swimming at first only in shallow water, with a flowing tide and a firm sand.
>
> It may be remarked that women—system and practice and other things being equal—usually make *better* swimmers than men, their lighter bones and softer outlines being better adapted for support and progress in the water. It is a charming sight to behold a whole family, properly dressed, disporting themselves round a raft or catamaran at the seaside.

Above: *Cassell's advice on swimming. Joyce grew sick of the 'moral message' and 'preaching' she found in the* Book of the Houschold.

Joyce seemed relaxed enough that evening. But when the children had gone back to school, and Paul to work, her feelings about returning to her corseted Victorian role became more aggressive. 'I'm supposed to be a good housekeeper,' she complained to her video diary, 'and a woman who cleans and cooks and that is her *raison d'être*. But I can't do that. OK, I can do it, but I don't want to do it. I think if I'd been around then I'd have been going to suffragette rallies. I feel like a rebel with a cause. This life as it is is making me extremely bolshy, angry, it's making me want to break out. I feel frustrated and trapped, rebellious, like when you're in your teens and you feel you want to change the world, that possibly you could, given the time and circumstances.'

Almost the thing that now enraged her most was Cassell's *Book of the Household*. 'I'm sick of the moral message, that you must do this, must do that. The preaching in it is so strong that when you've finished reading it you just end up feeling inadequate. Take this chapter about swimming. The whole thing is about men and boys, and then they give you this bit about women being lighter and so on. But they're not. Some women are built like brick shit-houses. You know, some women can play rugby or swim the Channel and yet here's Cassell's telling me all the time they can't. I think a hundred years ago a woman like me must have been slowly going mad. I don't know what she would have done. She'd have either hit the bottle or written a book.'

A couple of days later Joyce had become more philosophical about her situation. 'In bed, thinking,' she wrote in her diary. 'What's it all about when I am negative, childish and cross? It's not my true nature and I sound like a terrible moaner. Talking to Paul tonight I think we came upon a truth – that is, that in 1999 we feel that we have a right to be happy all the time. Whereas in 1900 there is less to make us feel happy. By 'happy' I don't just mean content or at peace with ourselves, I mean:

    1) Entertained.
    2) Stimulated.
    3) Inspired.
    4) Excited.

In other words almost delirious! The things which I said previously keep me sane – music, dancing, radio, etc. – maybe they are things which keep me HAPPY. It could be that I'm missing them more than I realised and therefore my mood changes are due to this. Was 1900 woman settling for less in the happiness stakes? Did she feel contented with the simpler things in life, i.e. feeling warm, feeling fed, feeling healthy? We are so lucky not to have to rely on basics such as those to supply our happiness. Or are we? Would I be a happier, saner person if I said to myself, "Life is sweet. I am not cold. I am not hungry. I am not ill. Those around me are in an equal position. I do not have to worry or despair for those I love, as they are not cold, hungry or unwell also. Life is good." Basically I have become a spoilt brat of a 1999 woman. I feel ashamed. Truly I do. To think I ranted and raved over such petty bloody things. Even the whole shampoo thing is so ridiculous. I think that my Victorian counterpart would not have understood me at all. She'd have said, "What's the bother about? She's got good money coming in every week, a hardworking husband, five strong healthy children, lovely clothes, food on the table and fuel in the range. She has a bathroom! She has a piano!" But in 1999 we do behave as if we have the right to have these things. I didn't regard myself as particularly materialistic, but I do now. I have discovered that I am as guilty as the next person when it comes to wanting things, wanting them now and wanting them the way I want them. I need to look at life differently as a 1900 woman. I need to slow down. I need to reappraise what is/isn't important. I've been so ARROGANT assuming that I know best, that I'm the one with all the answers. I have a lot of learning to do about the 1900 woman. I suspect that she can teach me some valuable lessons regarding what is and isn't important in life. Is it corny or trite to say that I've got my priorities all wrong and I need to look again at what I really need to be happy? I need to feel the reality of life as it was for the Joyce Bowler of 1900 and I do need to leave behind the Joyce Bowler of 1999. It has taken me four weeks to reach this point. This journey is a strange one.'

From her perspective, Hilary had been reaching similar conclusions. 'I think,' she confided to her video diary, 'a girl in 1900 would have been able to cope, because she would have been brought up like this. She would have known where everything was. She would have known how to do the washing, because she would have done it when she was younger, grown up with it. What I'm trying to say is that this 1900 girl would have known everything. And she wouldn't have had to go to a new school or if she did she would have fitted in, because everyone else would have been Victorian. She would have had friends outside that were Victorian, everyone down the street would have been Victorian, not just us, who are re-enacting it.

'I mean,' she went on, developing her theme, 'I would like someone who I can talk to, a friend of my age. If we don't have another Victorian family to speak to, we don't feel right.'

Kathryn was not so philosophical. 'The house is really depressing,' she complained. 'I've been hating every minute of it. I get on everybody else's nerves because I'm irritable. It's just not working out.' She was still missing her friend Sharon and her home social life of clubbing and going out. 'She's back home doing that,' she continued, 'and I'm stuck here and it just makes me hate the place even more. It just feels like a prison and I forget all my reasons for actually coming here in the beginning. I wanted us all to be a family, living in the house, because at home we hardly ever get to see each other. Hilary, Ruth and Joe are off at school, and Mum and Dad are normally out the whole weekend, and I thought it would be really nice – but to be quite honest I hate it. I really do. We're all on top of each other, having finickerty little fights and bickering for no reason whatsoever.

'I really wanted to do this project because of the adventure, but now I miss so much what I thought I wouldn't miss – my communication with my friends.' So much so that Kathryn had taken to using a local phonebox on her way back from college. 'I just had this massive temptation,' she confided. 'It was there, so I went in and spent about two or three quid of the money I brought up with me, just talking to Sharon, just about rubbish really, what she'd done today and what had happened in *EastEnders* and things like that.

'I miss my music as well. I did a very very sad thing the other day. I was in Lewisham and decided to have a break after college and go and look around the shops, give myself a bit of the twentieth-century world. I went to a clothes shop and they had some sort of dance music on, quite loud, and I was standing there thinking, OK, I'm not going to dance, I'm not going to dance. And I had to physically stop myself from dancing, it was really really sad, because normally, my friends know me, I'm a bit mental when we go out. But then I thought I looked a bit stupid because I started dancing on the shop floor. I had to quickly run away because everyone was looking at me, so it was a bit embarrassing.'

The person who was undoubtedly happiest in 1900 was, paradoxically, Paul, who had only agreed to do the project in the first place because of Joyce. 'I think we are getting into our pattern of life quite well now,' he told his video diary. 'I'm enjoying myself and I think everybody else is too. The range is working wonderfully and Joyce has been doing quite a lot in the kitchen to do with her corset and her hair. The girls are fine. Kathryn is now working at Charlie's Apples and Oranges and she's really enjoying that. I've let Hilary and Ruth go on a bus by themselves to the library in Blackheath. We are now members, though regulated on the sort of books we can have. They are eating up all the children's books that were pre-1900.

'I'm still interested in doing some exercise, like swimming, or even cycling, but I don't know what bicycles we'd use or where we'd go. Six bikes trundling down the main road, with all these

Above: *Paul, Joyce and Ruth on the train.*
On an Easter Monday trip to Forest Hill Joyce found
the behaviour of some of the passengers hard to take.
But later trips proved less stressful, and the family
grew used to the occasional questions about their
unusual appearance.

cars, it's a bit of a nightmare. We'd have to have safety helmets under our bonnets and stuff, so that would be quite interesting to see.'

The new moustache he had decided to grow was doing well. 'I am going to persevere with it,' he told his video diary. 'It may even need a little trim, it's a bit long over my lips, so I'm going to look in Cassell's and see if there is anything about looking after your moustache. I know there is wax in the medicine cabinet, but I don't know how to apply it.'

On the Thursday, to cap it all, it was his birthday. 'I'm having a lovely birthday,' he told his video diary. 'I've had some lovely presents, I've had toffee and I've got a pom pom and I've got a lovely picture from Hilary and a beautiful brass boat, and it's all very nice and I'm doing the things I want to do and I've just decided to have a go at cutting the grass with my lovely shears.'

The family rounded off the week with a trip to the circus, which was, Paul said, 'fantastic'. 'I can see,' he told his video diary, 'why the Victorians loved going to the circus, it was just wonderful, and nice to talk about something else but the house.' 'A fabulous time,' Joyce agreed. 'Exciting and enthralling, the clowns were funny, the acts were amazing, we oohed and aahed in all the right places, two hours of sheer bliss. Kathryn is off to run away with the daring young man on the flying trapeze. I'm not sure what I will do, but it'll involve something very tight and spangly.'

Hiring a servant

In 1900 the great majority of middle-class households employed at least one servant, a maid-of-all-work. Over ten per cent of the female population were listed in the 1901 census as engaged in 'indoor domestic service'. Most of them lived in, although by the turn of the century many households with one or few maids also engaged the services of a charwoman and/or a 'step boy' to assist with some of the domestic chores. Given the proximity in which families lived with their servants, care had to be exercised in choosing.

Servants were best engaged either through a local registry or a local newspaper. Most household guides of the period warned against agencies with exorbitant signing-on fees – all too often such agencies would take your money and fail to come up with any suitable servants. A nominal sum of one shilling was considered the maximum booking fee to be paid in advance; a further sum could be paid once a satisfactory maid had been provided.

Mistresses were advised to arm themselves, when interviewing prospective servants, with a list of questions – including the inevitable, 'Why did you leave your last position?' A servant was also expected to present a written reference, or 'character', from a previous employer. These, however, were often so conventionally worded as to be almost useless. Different authorities recommended different methods of making a truer assessment of a servant's capabilities. One writer in the American Kitchen Magazine *for 1899 advised the phrenological approach: 'In choosing a servant, see that the applicant's head extends back some distance behind the ears. This portion of the head is known as the "domestic region" and where it is not well developed, a servant is likely to be unsteady and dissatisfied. See also that the bump of firmness on the apex of the head rises well above the region of self-esteem, directly behind it. Otherwise the servant may prove insubordinate, independent, and altogether unpleasant.'*

A maid-of-all-work

In 1900 a family like the Bowlers would have had, not servants, but a maid-of-all-work. For some time now Joyce had been speculating about how the novelty of actually employing someone might work out. She had read the chapter on *Mistress and Servant* in Cassell's. 'This talks about mutual respect,' she wrote in her diary, 'and not commanding or ordering the poor old servant about. Will I give her the rotten dirty jobs? Mind you, I think there are enough for two, so I don't think we'll run out of things to do. It'll be nice to have someone to talk to but I am worried about the whole servant–mistress thing. Lots of people do have cleaning ladies (I've worked as a mother's help and nanny) so it isn't unheard of. Apparently I should supply a plan for her weekly work.

'Oh gawd,' she continued, after studying Cassell's a bit further. 'What are my priorities for a good servant?

1) Even-tempered, cheerful.
2) GSOH.
3) Not afraid of hard work.
4) Good at keeping confidences.
5) Bloody marvellous person.
6) Not a know-it-all.
7) Not too fussy about anything much at all.

Sounds like an ad in the Lonely Hearts column!'

Five applicants answered the little advert placed in the local paper, offering the job of cleaner for a television company, but only two turned up for interview. Joyce was a little disappointed not to meet the New Zealand rugger player who had applied. But in the end they were very happy with Elizabeth Lillington, a Peckham woman of Glaswegian origins, who came, she said, from four generations of professional cleaners and was, as Joyce observed, 'tall enough to reach things'.

Joyce was still concerned about how she should behave with her new servant. 'It's terrible,' she explained, 'because I keep thinking, "We can get loads done, Elizabeth and I." Then I'm thinking, "I'm not supposed to be doing it with her, am I?" She's supposed to be doing it for me. I'm paying her to do it, therefore I'm supposed to be doing other things, so possibly my hands will begin to heal, the cracks and sore skin may go away, perhaps I'll be able to do some sewing on the sewing machine. If I was musically inclined I could sit and play the piano. With the thought that at the end of it, when she goes home, I can come upstairs and look around and it will all be clean, like magic. Which is exactly what my little electrical slaves do for me in 1999. I load up the washing machine, I go to work, I come back, it's done. But I feel more comfortable about having an electronic device do it for me than a human being. Though of course in 1900 the thought around was that I was giving someone gainful employment, so instead of this poor woman having to walk the streets and starve I was actually employing her.

'So I want to be a benevolent employer. While I'm not actually going to clean up before she arrives, because that's mad, I suppose I'll be giving her cups of tea, free access to the outside toilet – I mean what else can I give her, there aren't really a lot of perks to this job. As much fluff as you can take home!'

After Elizabeth's first day, complete with nineteenth-century clothes, Joyce was delighted. 'She's fabulous,' she reported that evening. 'The house looks extremely clean and I am starting to feel freer inside. I'm starting to think, "Ooh, I can be a lady who lunches, I can go to my suffragette rallies, I can go to lectures."'

Elizabeth was now experiencing what Joyce had been through at the start of the project. 'I am absolutely exhausted,' she reported to one of the video diaries after her first day. 'All I've done is the stairs and brushing the dust under the bed. It took an hour and a half to brush the stairs and mop them, well not mop them, because we don't have a mop, but literally wash it down on hands and knees. I can't believe that women used to do this with a corset on, because I can hardly breathe, it is so impossible to keep bending down and brushing and then going back over it with a cloth, it's really hard work. I'm ready to go to bed now and it's only one o'clock in the afternoon.'

Seeing Elizabeth at work gave Joyce pause. 'I don't come from a privileged background,' she mused, 'I come from – if you've got to label it – some kind of working class. I come from south London, from intelligent people who have no money, no background, little or no education, no contacts. So a hundred years ago Joyce would have been the girl that came and scrubbed your floor.' Indeed, she went on, her own great-aunt Kate, whom she'd known as Auntie Kit, had worked as a scullery maid for Sir

A servant's day

The household guides for the period give vivid accounts of the expected daily duties of a maid in a single-servant household.

The maid should be up and ready by six o'clock in the summer and six-thirty in the winter. She should open the shutters, windows and doors. She should then clean the kitchen range and light it along with the other fires.

The cleaning of the front doorstep, the filling of the coal scuttles, and the polishing of the boots and the knives might be accomplished by a 'step boy', but if there wasn't one the work must be done by the maid. The maid must then wake the household, taking hot water up to the bedroom washstands. While the family is rising, she must dust the dining-room and lay the breakfast table, brush the hall and stairs, and then prepare the breakfast. Breakfast should be served at about eight o'clock. After the meal, the breakfast things must be cleared away and washed up, and the kitchen made tidy, ready for ten o'clock when the mistress will come there to give her orders for the day.

The maid should then 'attend to the bed rooms', emptying the chamber pots and carrying down the slop pails, before embarking on the 'special duty' of the day, as indicated by the mistress of the house. It might be a thorough cleaning of one of the rooms, or a beating of the carpets.

Having accomplished this, she should prepare lunch and lay the table in the dining room. If guests are coming to lunch, she should change into more formal attire and wait at table. If no guests are expected, the change of dress can wait until after lunch has been eaten, cleared and washed up.

From three o'clock onwards, if visitors are expected, she should attend to the front door, and bring afternoon tea into the dining room.

The next task – after the tea things have been removed – is to prepare dinner, to relay the table, cook the food, and wait if required. After this meal, eaten between seven and eight, the maid must clear it away, wash it up, and then put the kitchen in order. Her final chore was to prepare the bedrooms, putting hot water on the washstands, and turning down the beds.

It was a daily grind that allowed little time for rest or reflection; mistresses were advised always to keep their servants busy. The recommended amount of liberty was one evening per week between seven and ten o'clock, and the same time span on Sundays. Alternatively the whole of Sunday afternoon and evening might be taken off, in place of the evening in the week. Ten to fourteen days' holiday were suggested as being adequate. And the wages for all this – which of course included board and lodging – were between £18 and £26 per annum.

Above: *Elizabeth Lillington, the maid, at work with the carpet sweeper in Joe's bedroom. Elizabeth had strong private opinions on the way the house was run.*

Stafford Cripps. (In line with his socialist beliefs, he had been 'quite a benevolent employer, and allowed his servants access to the library'.)

'But look what's happened in a hundred years. Joyce is a girl that went to the local school, then on to grammar school and then was allowed by society, by everybody, was funded, because she had the intelligence, to go on and get a further education.'

A lady who lunches

Freed up by her maid-of-all-work, Joyce took a trip into town to see the Millais exhibition at the National Portrait Gallery. She was accompanied by her sister Katrina, who was visiting. This time the experience of going out was not a bad one. 'No one pointed,' Joyce wrote in her diary, 'laughed, was abusive or intrusive. All I was asked directly was, "Do you know the way to Chelsea?" To which I could answer, honestly, "No."'

She loved the exhibition. 'The paintings and drawings were beautiful. Some which captured me were those of the older Mr Gladstone, Lillie Langtry and a poor soul who committed suicide at thirty-eight. I do love to visit art galleries but as a mock-Victorian the thrill of it all is much heightened. We relish our entertainment much more as 1900 people than 1999 ones. Nowadays we have grown too used to constant stimulation. The shows, the TV programmes, books, everything must be more shocking and explicit, more TITILLATING than the last.

Above: *Having expressed an interest in photography, Paul was provided with a half-plate camera. Ruth was given a simpler Box Brownie, invented in 1900.*

'I don't want to sound pretentious, but you could see from the portraits what the people were actually like. There was this one small thin portrait of Ethel Ruskin. It said she was wearing the garment that was her habitual day dress. Now normally I would have just read that and thought nothing about it. But because I wear these things day in, day out as a Victorian, it really brought home to me the fact that she probably did, the whole time they were up in Scotland, wear this outfit.'

Afterwards the sisters went to Liberty's for a cup of tea. 'There were some ladies sat to one side and I noticed how beautifully dressed they were, how lithe and slim they appeared. I mean I can remember feeling like that and I don't feel like that now. I feel fat and lumpy, constricted, dirty. I turned to my sister and said, "Do I smell?" She told me I didn't, but it was very odd, because I'm only washing with soap and water, not wearing any deodorant, or perfume or body lotion.'

Though Joyce managed to resist the temptation and not look at Katrina's newspaper, she couldn't help visiting a 1999 chemist. 'We went in and she allowed me a full perusal of the whole hair-care range. I picked up the bottles, read the labels, had a good look, put them all back, came out – I was really proud of myself. I had a fabulous day.'

But by Wednesday the holiday was over. Elizabeth was ill with a throat infection. Secretly Joyce wondered if she would ever return. 'On a purely selfish level I hope she does come back, because she was fabulous.'

Paul, meanwhile, had been provided with a half-plate camera as part of the experiment. Chris Ridley, the stills photographer on the project, had shown him how to use it. Paul and

Above: *Paul adjusts the focus on his half-plate camera. At the front of the 'bellows', the fixed lens slides back and forwards on brass runners.*

Top: *The twins, meanwhile, pose patiently with doll and easel. For a satisfactory picture, they needed to remain still for five long seconds.*

Opposite: *Paul's photo of his daughters. Hilary described her father as 'completely obsessed' with his new hobby.*

Chris made a temporary darkroom out of the bathroom and Paul learned how to develop a glass negative and produce a positive image. Not to leave the children out, Ruth had also been given a Box Brownie, first available in 1900. Father and daughter were now all set to keep their differing, authentically period records of the second half of the 1900 House experiment. 'Dad's just completely obsessed now,' observed Hilary. 'The photos are going to be brilliant.'

An important visitor

For some time now the family had been looking forward to the visit of Daru Rooke, the social historian who had supervised the transformation of the house and decided on its contents. Joyce was, frankly, rather nervous. 'I hope that Daru doesn't resent our presence,' she wrote in her diary. 'I don't know why I'm saying this because he was saying such lovely positive things to us and he is such a gentle and sensitive person. But I worry: Are we the 1900 family he would like to see living in Elliscombe Rd? He is passionate about this experiment and I don't want to let him down. Does that seem silly?'

Meanwhile both she and her daughters were planning an entertainment for after the big dinner they were going to cook for their visitor. The twins were going to put on a short play about a ghost called Alice who was, Hilary explained, a little girl who had lived in the house in Victorian times. 'The whole play is based on her. First of all we've got the starting bit, that's scene one, where Mum and Dad are in the kitchen listening to Daru talking about the range and then pots keep flying everywhere and people get really cold. Then, scene two, we've got me and Ruth in bed and Alice comes out of the fireplace and starts playing with Ruth's doll. She moves its arms and tries to impersonate it, but she can't because she's dead and she can't work it out. Ruth and I wake up and see her as she flies off into the ceiling. Then she jumps onto the mantelpiece and looks into the mirror and I slowly get up and walk behind her and she's scared and she jumps off and I go, "Oh, are you hurt?" And she goes, "Nobody ever asked me that before. But it always hurts when I play with this doll." I ask why, and then she tells me that one day when she was playing with her doll, jumping up and down on the stairs, she fell down and that's why she comes out of the chimney because she's scared of stairs, because that's where she was dead. And then Ruth and I have got her, and we say, "Come on, Alice, come down the stairs," and we have this little song, where she's hopping down the steps. And there is a sort of moral to the story, it's to do with this project as well, it's if you take things one step at a time you'll get through it. Like if Mum and Dad can learn to take things one step at a time we'll get through the three months.'

Joyce and Kathryn, meanwhile, were working on an improving drama of their own. In her diary Joyce wrote out her draft script.

'My Script (plus AD LIBS)

Ladies and Gentlemen,
Here I stand before you a woman of the year 1900. Womanhood
personified! A picture of all a modern lady of our times could wish to be!

Or am I? Please close your eyes and cast your minds into the future, one hundred years away to the year 2000. Ladies and gentlemen, I give you the woman of the year 1999, as she enters the next Millennium in the year 2000.
(Applause as Kathryn enters.)

This is my manifesto for the woman of the future. By the year 2000 women will have:
1) Got the vote.
2) Got into parliament.
3) Come out again for a nice cup of tea.
4) Gone in again to give everyone What-for!
5) Invented a lovely stuff to wash hair which leaves it all soft and shiny.
6) Invented a way of washing dishes without getting their hands all dry and sore. *(Kathryn holds up PLACARD: Get a man to do it.)*
7) Bought bigger wardrobes to hold more clothes.
8) Bought more clothes.
9) Got the right to hold public office.
10) Got the right to choose which colour goes with their hair (whatever colour their hair may be that week!)
11) Restructured their whole wardrobe to go with the colour of their hair.
12) Spent years in selfless research into effective anti-ageing creams and lotions in the search for a scientific breakthrough which will help all other women.
13) Discovered one which works and decided not to share this secret with all other women.
14) Decided that, well, we can't have it all, don't want it all but it's JUST SO NICE to have the choice should we really want to.

Yes, ladies and gentlemen, here she is, Miss Year 2000. But don't despair gentlemen, she won't neglect you and no doubt she will still have a place in her heart for a military man.

SONG
Fin'

Elizabeth had by now recovered from her viral infection and was back at work. The maid-of-all-work had started her own written diary and was somewhat critical of her employer's cleaning efforts. 'The main room looked clean enough,' she wrote, 'until I touched the ornaments and water bowl which was all covered in thick dust. The two small rooms were thick with dust, especially the floors, which being without carpets had at least two inches of dust under the bed. She is not coping with the housework at all.'

Nonetheless, she and Joyce got on well. 'I admire her a lot,' Elizabeth wrote, and then a day or two later, 'We have become friends, rather than employer and maid. She did tell me,' she added, 'that she feels embarrassed that I am there to clean for her and really she should be embarrassed as the house is filthy.' A day later she wrote, 'She admitted to me that she only brushed the stairs once by hand and it nearly killed her, she just isn't used to physical work, she is more of an intellect.'

'Today,' Elizabeth wrote on the Thursday, 'I spent most of the morning cleaning and polishing as Joyce has told me that tomorrow they are expecting a visitor who is an historian. He is an expert on the social history of the 1900s. Joyce is nervous and excited at the same time. She's said this is because he is an expert, but really she is the one who has become expert. She is living the history that he is studying.'

The big day

'The Big Day' Elizabeth headed her diary entry. She got the breakfast dishes out of the way while Paul and Joyce prepared the parlour for Daru Rooke's arrival. Then mistress and maid discussed what they were going to cook for dinner: tomato and vegetable stew with spaghetti, followed by rhubarb custard, meringues, banana fritters and sponge cake.

The morning was spent cleaning. 'Then at 2 p.m. exactly.' Elizabeth wrote, 'Daru arrived. He looked immaculate, dressed in a black suit with a yellow cravat. I answered the door to him. "Good afternoon, sir," I said, "won't you come in." He came into the hall. I then asked him if he had a calling card. He replied, "No." Then he asked if Mr and Mrs Bowler were at home. I made him wait in the hall while I told Paul that he had a visitor. They then came into the kitchen for their tea. I had everything prepared for them and the three sat round the table for a chat. I stayed in the scullery.

> ## To clean enamelled saucepans
>
> *In an age before Fairy Liquid and plastic pan scourers, washing-up was a more complicated business: 'In cleaning enamelled saucepans, wash inside and out with hot water and soda. Then scour with a mixture of salt and fine sand, two parts sand to one of salt. Rinse with hot water and dry.'*
> Madge's Book of Cookery

'They talked of how they were getting on. Daru asked how they were coping. Straightaway Paul answered saying he was handling it OK and enjoying it. Joyce said the opposite. She said while she was finding the life fascinating, it was also much harder than she had anticipated.

'Then I was introduced properly to Daru, who is a most charming and interesting man. I wanted to ask him if in fact a maid-of-all-work would have worn a corset while working. I was a bit disappointed when he said yes, as it is very uncomfortable to work in. He explained that if, a hundred years ago, I would have lived at the house, I would most likely have slept on the floor in the kitchen and been fed on scraps. He painted a very dire picture of a maid's life. He went on to say that I would have perhaps come from the country where there was no work. I would not have known anyone in the city, which is what my employers would have liked, and I would have tried to better myself by learning domestic skills and perhaps met the butcher or baker boy who may have become my husband. I wondered if I would have been taught to read and write, but Daru said probably not as I would have received basic education at the village school.'

Elizabeth and Joyce had already planned the preparation of the dinner, bearing in mind such logistic difficulties as the fact that water still took half an hour to boil on the range. By

5.30 they were ready. 'Paul came in and wanted to know what he should do. I told him I could manage but he insisted on getting the water ready. I realised that he had a small chip on his shoulder as I am doing all the jobs that he would have done. Eventually Joyce sent him off to lay the table – what a relief, he was out of the kitchen! I started on the batter. I was scared of the outcome as I'd never made banana fritters in the 1990s, let alone in 1900.

'When the table was set it looked really lovely. The youngest child Joe threw a wobbler and refused to get his clean shirt on. I grabbed him by his arm and dragged him upstairs and all the way he was punching me, but I had him by the neck so he wasn't hitting me too hard. By the time I got him to his room he was fine and ready to change. We were having a laugh when Paul came in and ordered me out of the room and reprimanded Joe. It was totally unnecessary. He blew it all out of proportion and made himself look ridiculous. I let it wash over my head as it is not my business to interfere. I carried on with the cooking and when the family was ready and seated I served the food. The spaghetti was sticky and Joyce said it was a stupid idea to serve it at the table but it wasn't my idea, it was the TV director's. By this time I was fed up with the moaning and wished they would get on with things and relax. I mean, I was having fun and I was doing all the work so what was their problem? I served up the main course and everything was fine, apart from Paul calling me every minute to ask for things I had already taken care of. To make matters worse Joe kept calling me "Maid". I got the feeling he would have made my life hell if this was a real-life situation. If he was my child he would have got put over my knee and spanked.

'Once the main course was finished and cleared away by me I served pudding. All in all, everything went really well and I was looking forward to the entertainment, but the dishes kept piling up. It took me twenty minutes to wash and dry the main dishes and pots.

'Once the entertainment started I put on my best apron and waited in the kitchen. I waited and waited, then Paul called me in. I was happy to be invited, but

The dinner party

There were strict rules for all formal occasions in the 1900 household. An event such as a dinner party had to be carefully planned and executed. Social commentators had firm views on what was to be served and how it was to be done. There was a fashion in these things. And the fashion of 1900 was for the so-called dinner à la russe – 'the Russian style' in which all the dishes were taken round by a servant and handed to each guest in turn. The earlier fashion had been to place all the dishes on the table, and have them served by the host and hostess, but in the new style only decorations and candles were allowed on the table.

The number of dishes prescribed by the experts was imposing. According to the leading authorities the meal should begin with soup, and then fish. These preliminaries should be followed by the entrées, a series of 'small made up dishes… such as cutlets, scallops, curries, quenelles, &c.'. After this diversion should come the joints of meat, then a roast game-bird, then a dish of vegetables. Various sweet dishes – ices, jellies or fritters – should be served next; these might be followed by a cheese soufflé. Then came the dessert of fresh fruits. Sherry, claret and champagne should be served to accompany the meal.

Only after all this was the hostess permitted to lead the other ladies of the party into the drawing-room for coffee. The men remained at the table, to drink their port and receive their coffee, before rejoining the ladies.

A slight flexibility was allowed. Some experts recommended the American innovation of serving the joints before the entrées, feeling that it was advisable to fill the guests up with plain rather than fancy fare. Another common suggestion was to serve the vegetable dishes between the joint and the game, rather than after the latter.

The whole scheme of the meal was excessively elaborate. It was borrowed from the conventions of aristocratic society, and humble middle-class households struggled to replicate it. By dining à la russe they involved themselves in the expense of hiring a servant specially for the occasion. The number of dishes placed a great strain on the capability of both their cook and their range. The more practical household guides, such as Cassell's, constantly urged moderation. 'The great secret of successful household dinner-giving is not to attempt too much. A few courses well cooked are far better than many courses indifferently cooked, and it is far easier to entertain a few friends than it is to entertain a crowd. Indeed, it is better in every way to give two small parties than a single large one.'

he only wanted me to make the tea, which I did and still no invite. I spent the rest of the evening on my own in the kitchen cleaning up. I could hear them all laughing and clapping. My feet

Above: *Paul's photo of Daru Rooke's visit to Elliscombe Road. After all his hard work creating the 1900 House, Joyce was concerned not to let Daru down.*

were aching, my back hurt and my hands were red raw, and although everyone thanked me and said I did a great job, I would have been more grateful if I was invited to join in like a member of the family. I did not ever think I would not be invited in, as Joyce has always said she would never have a maid or get used to one being in her house, yet here I am two weeks into the work and her husband is treating me like a real skivvy.

'It changed my attitude towards the family and I felt rather sad for the young girl who would have done my work a hundred years ago, as she would have had nowhere to go. The house would have been her life and it must have been very hard and lonely for her, always being treated as if she was beneath her master. If she was unlucky enough not to be able to afford books I do not think she would have had any escape from the grim reality of her life.'

Elizabeth, however, had been the only one to have a disappointing time on that splendid evening. 'It's five past eleven at night,' an excited Joyce confided to her video diary later. 'I'm trying not to shout because everyone's in bed. I've just taken my corset off, after seventeen hours of wearing it, so I think I've broken my own record. I've had a fabulous day. Really, really nervous before Daru came, because I wanted it to be interesting for him. And satisfying. To know that all his work in preparation was appreciated and was being used. I just wanted to speak to him again really and share everything with him.

'I was nervous about the meal, about getting everything just right, making sure the children were happy about their entertainments, which I must say went down so well. I was so proud of them. They were all fantastic. And our wonderful maid who was shoving plates down and snatching them up and doling out the food – it was just an absolute scream, from start to finish.

'I think Daru has had a good day. Seeing him brings home to me all my hopes and dreams about the whole enterprise. I've created a fairytale land for myself where this is where I live and you know, we really are living the 1900 life.'

Kathryn was equally enthusiastic about both evening and guest. 'I didn't think this evening would go very well,' she confided, 'because nothing was very much

Mutual Respect.—One thing is very certain: before we can establish this happy condition we must readjust the relations between the mistress and the servant, and each must take up a new attitude towards the other. For we may as well confess that the relation between domestics and their employers is not what it used to be. The old patriarchal relation is a thing of the past. Some years ago it was understood that the mistress was a sort of guardian to the servant, and had absolute control over her in every way; had a right to say how she should dress, and how she should spend her leisure. Servants have rebelled against this rule; they have asserted their rights, not always very judiciously or politely; and the consequence is that neither mistresses nor servants know fully where they are.

After thinking a good deal about the matter, the conclusion we arrive at is, that in readjusting the relations, the first thing to be done is for both mistresses and servants to resolve to respect one another's rights. This is the attitude which will have to be taken up if the domestic wheels are to run smoothly. Let it be understood that the two parties stand towards each other in the position, not of guardian and ward, or patron and dependent, but in the attitude of buyer and seller; and let us see how this will work. The servant's stock-in-trade is her ability and willingness to do certain work, in a certain way, at certain hours. The mistress has the right to say how and when the work shall be done, and also has the right to lay down certain rules of domestic management, which rules should be set down " in the bond." But with the observance of these rules her rights end, and the servant's rights have possession of the field. The mistress may and should try to influence on the ground of their common humanity; but she has no claim to command.

Above: *Joyce was concerned about the relationship between mistress and servant.* Cassell's *Book of the* Household *gave her advice about 'mutual respect'.*

planned and it was all a bit iffy. But we got there and it was fantastic. He was a really good audience. I never had the chance to really talk to him before, but he's a really, really nice person. He's so talented and I wish we stay in contact because he's a fantastic man.'

Daru had enjoyed the day. 'I've had a fantastic time,' he confided to Joyce and Paul's video, 'being entertained by the family. The whole place just seems a lot cosier than it did when I was last here. It seems like a proper home now, as they've moved everything and changed everything to meet their needs. It's really, really lovely. I did find Mr Bowler's impersonation of a kangaroo difficult, because he didn't impersonate the joey as the rest of his family pointed out, but apart from that it's been great and I'm looking forward to having a good night's rest away from the television, radio and telephone. 1900's pretty good, really.'

In the Swim

On the Sunday after Daru's visit Paul took the family swimming at Greenwich Arches Leisure Centre. Or most of the family. Unfortunately it was Joyce and Kathryn's time of the month so they had to stay behind 'feeling a bit disgruntled'; fantasising about how many lengths they would have swum and what it would have been like in Victorian costumes; pretending to be a Mexican and a Swede; dancing and playing 'every indoor game known to humanity'; inventing scenarios for the two china dogs from the mantelpiece, Percy and Stinky; going out to the Co-op to buy some envelopes; filming each other with the video cameras; conjuring up ideas of the man Kathryn would eventually marry ('old, rich and darkly handsome') and generally getting bored. 'We're alienated,' Joyce mused. 'Why? All because we're women. We're outcasts from

Below: *The costumes worn by Paul, the twins and Joe, were authentic to the period. When Joyce finally got to try them, she found them 'extremely clinging and heavy'.*

Opposite: *The Bowler family swimming at Greenwich Leisure centre. The outing was proclaimed to be 'a great day' by Ruth.*

society. We would have liked to have gone swimming, but we can't. And there's nothing more to be said, really. Just our lot, and we're meant to put up with it.'

The others, meanwhile, were having all the fun Joyce was imagining. 'It was really good to be out and about and free,' Ruth reported later. 'The swimming costumes were nice fitting when they were dry. Once you got a bit wet they stuck to you, totally. We had to jump in a few times and every time I jumped in the bit on my collar flicked up into my face, it was like you were being attacked by these frilly things.

'Anyway, we did lots of games like going under people's legs and races underwater and it was really fun. We had lots of exercise which you need to burn off the excess fat and stuff, so it was a great day out.'

'My costume,' Paul reported, 'fitted me like a triathlon suit. It was slightly hairy, but once in the water it was great. The rest of my clothes are so stiff and straight, and this was about the skimpiest thing I've got in my wardrobe. It seemed very, very not-Victorian.

'Half of the centre is a leisure pool, built for kids, with slides and things, and then on the right-hand side is an old, what I would call Victorian, pool. It's got a beautiful, like, stage area right at the back, and it's got a beautiful mural painted on there of a Victorian seasidey picture. It's got cubicles on either side and it just smelt wonderful. I couldn't wait to get in there.

'I got in the water and it was wonderful. Just such a release on what I'd been wearing and the environment we'd been in. I haven't done any formal exercise since we started all this. It was wonderful just to stretch and exercise my muscles.

'But on reflection Joyce and Kathryn didn't come, which was quite sad. I do believe they have missed quite a treat and I feel sort of down on that. Because when we got home, you could see it in their faces. For one thing we were very clean, having been in the pool for about two and a half hours, and you could see they'd missed it. In fact, Joyce was slightly off with us. I do seem to land the cake and the cherry every time.

'All right, there's a hint of jealousy there, but I just hated leaving them behind, I really did. I wish they'd come as spectators. But if I say that to her now she will probably get quite cross. Oh dear, I feel guilty, yet I really enjoyed myself. I just want to say, "Joyce, you will get your chance, and I'm sorry it didn't happen now."'

It just seemed to be Paul's lot to have his good intentions misunderstood. Back in her flat Elizabeth was still musing bitterly on the events of Friday night. 'I find the more I consider the treatment I received from Mr Bowler the more angrier I get, and realise that it was his attitude that made his son act in such a rude way.'

Really living it

Paul's temporary job with the Royal Marines Careers Centre in Kensington had now come to an end. He was back to his regular job at Lympstone in Devon, which meant being away from the house for three days each week. One aspect of her husband Joyce didn't pine for was his Victorian facial hair. 'I am sick of Paul's moustache,' she told her video diary. 'Honestly, he comes towards me to kiss me and it's like being advanced on by somebody with a bristle brush, a yard brush. It's horrible, very nasty, so I'm hoping he's going

to get rid of that before the end of our time here. How can I convince him that it would be a good idea to shave it off?'

For Joyce, otherwise, 1900 life had settled into a routine. 'The days trot on,' she wrote in her diary, 'and life goes on and time passes. I feel that we are well into the 1900 House experience now, not pretending or trying to do it, but really living it.

'At the core of the experience is the range, which I feed, rake, riddle and tend regularly all day. At night I prepare it well so that it will stay on all night and Paul and I take turns to get up first and see if it's still "in". These days it *is* without fail and that means hot water for Paul's shave, boiling water for the tea, and a fire to cook porridge on.

'Life has a pattern and now that the maid comes in I am expected to amuse myself and spend my time as a middle-class lady of the time would. Of course she wouldn't have heard of radio, TV, George Michael, jazz, or any of the things which I miss. She would have visited friends, gone shopping, done good works, etc., which I find it difficult to do (not having the contacts or network of family and friends).

Above: *Watched by Kathryn, Joyce sews with her Singer. She did occasional running repairs to all the family's clothes, mended the twins' torn blouses and Joe's split trousers, as well making a pair of bloomers for Kathryn. She found that not a lot had changed since 1900 as far as a sewing machine was concerned; if anything the old Singer was an improvement on her modern machine, with fewer parts to go wrong.*

Above: *Joe prepares to collect eggs from the chickens' laying tray. The hen-house was an old Irish whiskey barrel, converted by Fred Hams, the chicken expert. From their initial training at Shugborough onwards, Joe was enthusiastic about the chickens. He made it his daily job to feed them and collect eggs.*

'It was bloody miserable not being able to go swimming on Sunday. I looked great in my costume, even if I do say so myself. I am considering wearing it every day, to escape the prison of being in a corset. Somehow I am afraid to take off the clothes – even for a day – because the spell will be broken and I wonder if I could ever put them on again.

'I wrote about the clothes being my time-travel device and I feel that they are. I feel, strongly, that if I was freed from the corset, the layers of petticoats and undies and the rest, then I would have left 1900 behind – and I long to leave it behind, because it is so difficult and so wearing. It never gets easier. Yes, it gets more familiar and routine, but that doesn't make it more bearable or fun. Victorian middle classes didn't get much fun. In fact, I doubt if that word is in their dictionary. Excuse me while I look it up.

'Oh good grief! It *isn't* in there. *Pears Cyclopaedia 1897* English dictionary section goes from Fumigate to Funambulist. Where's the FUN?'

Above: *Watched by Joyce and the family, Paul makes scrambled eggs. In general, Paul cooked breakfast, while Joyce prepared the evening meal.*

Kathryn wasn't feeling much better. 'I didn't want to get out of bed this morning,' she told her video diary, 'because I couldn't be bothered to put on that horrible corset and those horrible smelly dirty clothes, which make you look like you've got a massive belly and bum. Eventually I managed to get out of my nightdress and over my slight depression and out in the sunshine. That is the only thing that is keeping me going at the moment. Sunshine. Some sort of brightness in my life.

'I went to college for a couple of hours, came back, put my corset on again and whilst I was eating my tea, I'd eaten a sort of a few mouthfuls and I had a very strange feeling in my stomach. I went to the toilet and sicked it all back up again, it was absolutely disgusting. Obviously the food had got stuck where my corset goes in. It was horrible. Normal clothes don't make you sick, do they?'

Elizabeth the maid could hardly fail to notice the atmosphere. 'It is hard to go to work every day in a good mood to face depressed people,' she wrote. 'I have tried hinting at hobbies and the garden and such, but to no avail. Now I know Joyce keeps out of my way when I'm cleaning,

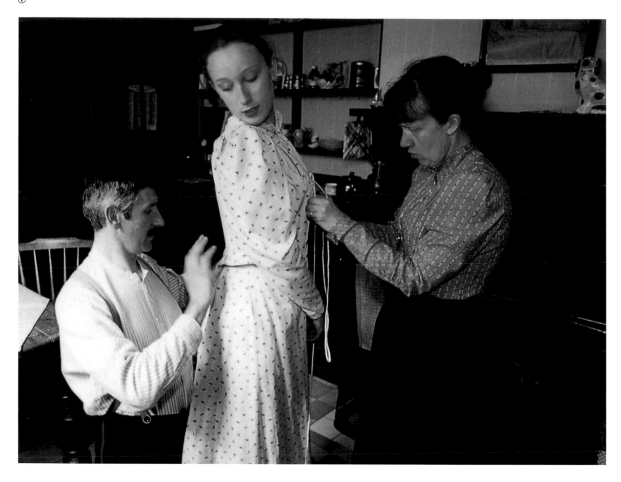

Above: *Paul and Joyce lacing Kathryn into a dress with a fitted corset. Eventually this restrictive garment made her physically sick.*

as she feels she should be doing it perhaps, but then she makes no effort to make my life easier by brushing a floor now and then, so I concluded that she has had enough of the good old bad old days and wants out. No stamina!!'

As for Elizabeth, she reminded herself that she had inherited the mental strength of her ancestors. 'When I'm working I think of the work my grandma did and I feel like I'm living in her shoes. Even though she worked very hard, she always said she would not swap places with the lady of the house, as the lady always looked weak and ill.'

Changing shape

But being the lady of the house brought its own problems, Joyce was discovering. 'Assertiveness,' she told her video diary one morning when Elizabeth had still not appeared for work at ten o'clock, 'comes in many shapes and forms and I'm afraid I don't think I've got it when it comes to reprimanding employees. I'm very new to this game and I haven't had a maid-of-all-work for very long. I was just thinking about what to say to somebody who is persistently half an hour late. I'm very good at telling people what to do, but I'm not very strong, and even if she didn't clean properly or whatever I'd probably just say, "Thank you very much" and pay up at the end of the week, which is a painful thing to admit really, that you're a spineless worm. I keep feeling like she's doing me a favour, but I should just remember that she's getting paid to do it.'

Elizabeth didn't turn up that day, so Joyce reverted to her working-class roots and did her own cleaning. 'It actually makes me feel better,' she wrote in her diary that night. 'I might work off some of this carbohydrate-sugar- and fat-based lumpiness.

'I am actually changing shape,' she decided, as she studied herself, corsetless, in the mirror. 'And so is Kathryn. We're both getting this silly little squashed-in ribby waist, an enormous bum and a distended belly. It's not attractive and it's not a shape I want to be. I'm sure in the year 1900 this was supposed to be voluptuous and gorgeous but we don't want to be gorgeous 1900 style. We want to go back to our normal bodies.

'And the other thing that has been happening to me now for quite some time, and I haven't told anybody, is that after I take my corset off in the evening, within five minutes, my bladder empties, all on its own. I don't have control of it and I'm really quite concerned. So what do I do? Do I spend the last few weeks of the experience wearing a Victorian swimming costume?'

But as the days went on and became increasingly fine, Joyce left her depression behind. 'A gloriously sunny day,' she wrote on Friday 30 April, 'I am happy. Paul is home and building the shed. All is well with my world as I sit in the garden and watch my hens being very entertaining. We have eleven eggs, all laid since 25 April.'

At the weekend Paul took her to her first ever football match: Charlton Athletic, the local team, versus Blackburn Rovers. 'I thought it was great,' she told her video diary, 'really exciting. I wonder why I've waited so long to do this. It's something I shall repeat again, a real high spot.' Joyce was delighted there had been no barracking from the crowd at their costumes; they were all concentrating far too hard on the game, she thought.

Now into the last month at the 1900 House, Joyce was starting to appreciate how special the experience was. A photograph her father sent her, of his father as

Corsets

Corsets of one type or another had been a feature of women's dress since the sixteenth century. It was thought desirable to pinch the female form into an exaggerated shape, to accentuate the fullness of the bust and the narrowness of the waist. The fashion was certainly in full force in 1900.

Corsets – or stays – made from wool or calico, into which blades of whalebone were inserted, were worn by most middle-class women. The corset, which covered most of the torso, had to be laced up from behind to squeeze in the wearer's waist. This 'tight lacing', as it was called, was both uncomfortable and unhealthy. But it was fashionable and, as a result, it was endured. There were, however, objections to the custom. From the 1880s onwards, in artistic circles, the 'Rational Dress Society' campaigned for less restrictive clothing. The society advocated flowing Pre-Raphaelite robes worn without stays. But the novelty and the bohemian flavour of these garments provoked more alarm than approval. Rational Dress was regarded by many as 'something outrageous and immodest', and the people who adopted it were condemned as wishing to 'make themselves singular and remarkable'.

Nevertheless even an authority as conservative as Cassell's Book of the Household *admitted the essential wisdom of the society's creed, while balking at the excesses of some of its members. Tight lacing was roundly condemned as both stupid and wicked: 'It not only ruins the health of those who practise it, but it throws a burden upon the next generation, and weakens the race. The heart, lungs and liver cannot possibly act properly if they are deprived of the room which was given to them by Nature; and this is one reason why there is so much indigestion, constipation and flatulence amongst women... It is a destroyer of beauty; it ruins the circulation and digestion, and through them the complexion. It is the cause of pimples on the face, of a red nose, of faintings, hysteria, and nervousness.'*

Despite these dire warnings the practice continued, largely unchecked, throughout the period. Indeed it did not really die out until the 1920s. The corset itself did change its form slightly over the Edwardian era; from about 1912 a shorter model was adopted. The breasts, which had previously been supported by the top of the corset, now had to have independent support – the brassière was introduced to provide it. The corset itself gradually transformed itself into the 'girdle'.

Above: *Paul and Joyce at a Charlton Athletic football match. Joe is wearing a Victorian football shirt under his authentic period braces.*

a young man in his Army uniform in the 1920s, prompted her to realise how much she had been missing. He was the 'dead spitting image' of her brother Toby and suddenly was so real to her. 'I remember going to Grandad's and eating winkles for tea and wondering why he was eating things out of a shell with a pin, but I'd never really thought of him as a real person. He was just Grandad. It's sad I didn't know him properly. I remember him saying they were given a house and got hot water just before the war, and Nan was really thrilled because she had running water. And this isn't so long ago, is it? Yet the amount of advances that have been made since then, they just blow you away. And I don't think we ever take them on board properly, we take so much for granted these days. We don't realise what's actually happened in the last hundred years. And I think if there was going to be any kind of celebration at the millennium, it should be all about this, where we've been and how far we've travelled, how far technology has taken us – not always in a good direction.

'Life has become so superficial. And what do we do with all the wealth of knowledge and the richness that older people have to share with us? We ignore it. They're not useful any more. They're not attractive, they don't play a worthwhile part in society, we think – yet they've got so much to teach us.

'This whole thing has just taken me apart and it's just shaken me. It's gone right to the core of my being and I feel immensely privileged to be having this experience.'

Votes for women!

While Joyce's spirits improved, maid-of-all-work Elizabeth got on with the daily cleaning of the house, keeping a careful record of her routine. 'Arrived at the house at 9.45. Lifted both rugs in the hall and kitchen and put them out on the washing line to be aired and later beaten. Mrs B. took me upstairs into the girls' room and told me she wanted the room spring cleaned. I undid the beds, shook the blankets and sheets and folded them away, moved all the furniture out of the room, moved the glass and chinaware into the bathroom to be washed later. I then sprinkled tea leaves onto the carpet and brushed it. I then rolled up the carpet and put it in the hall. I lifted the mattress ...'

Little wonder that by the weekend she was writing, 'Last week has practically left me with blisters. Now my hands are much harder than they were and after work it takes me a good fifteen minutes to clean them. If I had to do this work forever I should want on my grave the Tired Woman's Epitaph that goes like this:

> Here lies a poor woman, who always was tired;
> She done the work of four, but only she was hired
> Her last words on earth were,
> "Dear friends I am going
> Where washing ain't done, nor sweeping, nor sewing,
> But everything there is exact to my wishes,
> For where they don't eat, there's no washing of dishes.
> Don't mourn for me now, don't mourn for me never,
> I'm going to do nothing for ever and ever."

'Yesterday,' Elizabeth confided to Joyce's videos, 'I managed to get a book from the library about Victorian women and it's fascinating. I mean, I honestly didn't know that women used to work down the coal mines, eight hours a day in the pits, sometimes with bare feet. And the maid-of-all-work, she would be lucky if she got four or five hours' sleep a night.

'I think it's time they started teaching women's history at school, because they never taught me anything about women working like this. The impression I got was that in the 1950s, or whenever, it was ridiculous to think that women could even fix a plug or a lawnmower or something. But where does that come from, because a hundred years before that they were working in factories, down mines, doing practically everything that men could do. I'm really learning a lot now.'

It was ironic that Joyce, whose fascination with the history of women's liberation had begun somewhat earlier in the project, was now freed up by Elizabeth's cleaning efforts to take her interest further. In the middle of the week she took the train into town to the Museum of London at the Barbican, where she met Diana Dorrelly, whose grandmother had been the suffragette Myra Sadd-Brown. Joyce was able to see the archives of the Women's Social and Political Union and all kinds of material associated with the suffragette movement: posters, banners, songsheets, support badges, medals, even a tea-set in the suffragette colours of white, purple and green and badges from a Men's Support Group. The highlight was holding one of

Women's rights

Although full women's suffrage was not achieved until well into the twentieth century, the late-Victorian period did see a steady increase in women's rights and a steady expansion of women's roles.

There were legal victories, which gave women more control over their own property and persons. The improvements to the system of women's secondary and further education, achieved in the 1860s, not only brought benefits to female students but also opened up a world of educational employment for a whole generation of women.

Women also, for the first time, began to play a role in public life. The reforms to local government in the last years of the nineteenth century opened up many new spheres of public activity and inquiry – public health, education, sanitation, social welfare – and capable middle-class women were quick to involve themselves. Women's voices were heard for the first time on public platforms, and the subjects they chose to address were not always conventionally acceptable. They campaigned against unpopular measures such as vivisection, compulsory vaccination and the Contagious Diseases Act (which allowed for the compulsory and forced inspection of prostitutes suspected to be suffering from venereal disease). Women began to join political parties and to campaign in parliamentary elections; although, of course, they were not able to vote in them.

In 1900 the movement for women's suffrage was being orchestrated by the pioneering feminist Millicent Fawcett. Her National Union of Women's Suffrage Societies campaigned not only for the vote but also for a whole list of other social and economic measures. Perhaps there were too many items on the agenda. It was from the Fawcett group that Mrs Pankhurst and her supporters broke away in 1905. They felt that their message was getting diluted; they wished to pursue the quest for the vote with single-minded (if not always legal) rigour.

Not until 1918, however, was it granted to married women over thirty, and only in 1928 was it extended in line with male suffrage to all women over the age of twenty-one.

the leather belts that the suffragettes had used to tie themselves to London railings.

'There wasn't enough time,' she told her video diary later. 'I mean, I could happily have spent days and days there really, poring over it all and pulling everything out and having a good old look. I feel as if my brain has been set on fire by living here and doing these things. My life will never be the same again, the experience has touched me in ways I never ever dreamt of. For example, I really do want to belong to the Fawcett Society. So that I can pay my dues really. And continue the work that was started by these women that I really admire.

'It was a real privilege today to be able to see the exhibits and touch the things they used in their struggle. When I saw that broad leather belt with the chain-link additions, originally I thought it was something the authorities put on the women to restrain them when they were in prison. But no, it was something that a suffragette had actually made herself, so she could chain herself to the railings. To touch it just brought history alive for me.

'I've been wearing a corset every day for nearly three months, so I know what you feel like having your photograph taken in that get-up. And I like to think I know what they felt like, their sense of injustice and their struggle. When you understand how women were treated, how so very recently we were second-class citizens. We have come such a long way in such a short time, but then we still have a long way to go. There are lots of women who don't get equal pay for equal work, still. I'm not saying I want to be better than men, just on an equal footing.

'So I say a million thank yous to all the women who put everything on the line for me, their respectability, their status, their marriages, their future, their freedom, not just for the vote, but so that they could be seen as equal members of society.

'And let's have no more history at arm's length, behind glass cases. Let's make it live, make it real, so we understand where we've come from, and when a woman does get into Parliament, we realise how amazing that is.

'Young women need to know these things about our history: so they can be aware how very recently these changes have come about and have the confidence to carry it all forward. It's amazing how quickly we forget the struggle that went on earlier in the century. So no more young women, please, saying, "Oh, I don't think I'll bother to vote." You blimming well get down there and vote, you don't have to be a card-carrying member of a political party, but use your vote, even if it's just choosing the person with the most teeth, or the least revolting of your local candidates. Votes for women!'

'Liberating' Elizabeth

Relations between employer and maid had been good. Joyce felt mildly irritated when Elizabeth managed to break all Joseph's shirt buttons in the mangle; and Elizabeth had been angry when Paul had thrown away the tea leaves she had been collecting for two weeks to clean the carpets with, before giving her a lecture about how carpets *should* be cleaned. But by and large, with Paul away three days a week, they had been getting on fine.

'We can have some really close, good discussions,' Elizabeth observed one day. On another, when Elizabeth had taken her employer for a walk in the local park: 'Mrs B. was in a much better mood when I left, so I felt I'd earnt my pay.' On another: 'Mrs B. has fell into her role perfectly, it is really nice to see and live this, when I have read about it in a history context. I know I am really living history.'

But then one fine day in early May, Joyce finally got the chance to go swimming at Greenwich Leisure Pool – in a 'very snazzy' navy blue costume with a red and white trim. 'I didn't feel silly in it at all,' she wrote in her diary that evening, 'until I got out and then it was EXTREMELY clinging and heavy.'

Being in the water, however, was 'pure bliss'. 'Just the feeling of absolute, sheer, well, liberation. I've been imprisoned in these Victorian clothes for so long, it was just absolutely wonderful to be able to feel the warmth of the water and stretch out. While I was swimming about I started to think about having a maid and I suppose I was thinking about freedom, how lovely it was to have freedom and how it would only have been certain people who went swimming in 1900 and how, probably, the poor

The use of tea leaves

Old, slightly damp, tea leaves were often used when sweeping the carpets, as a means of binding the dust and making it easier to sweep up. There were, however, other uses for them:
'Tea leaves are invaluable for many purposes. Save the spent ones for three or four days, soak them in a tin pail for about an hour, then strain off the leaves through a sieve, and the tea water left gives a capital wash for all varnished paint. Window sashes and oil cloth should always be worked with it, and it is better than anything for window panes, looking-glass, and the glass of pictures. But it must not be used on unvarnished paintwork.'
Madge's Book of Cookery

little maid-of-all-work wouldn't have been able to go and I felt a real hypocrite, because on the one hand I'm saying, I don't really like having a maid, cleaning all my muck up, and then on the other, I leave all my breakfast dishes for her, because I know she's going to come.

'And yesterday she didn't come, because she wasn't well and I did all the dishes, all the things I'd been doing for the first month, and I felt so much better about it. So I've come to the conclusion I don't want a maid any more, because I feel it is hypocritical for me to be saying, "Isn't it terrible having someone waiting hand and foot on you," and what a dreadful lifestyle she would have had, and then I'm expecting someone to do it. So I'm going to have to let her go, I'm afraid.

'Now that leaves me feeling terrible, because I don't want to give her the sack, but it just doesn't feel right having a maid. I can't sit and watch her do the work, even if I'm sitting

Above: *Elizabeth Lillington at work. The maid didn't see her 'liberation' from Victorian drudgery in quite the same light as her employer.*

or sewing or reading, it's like: Why the hell aren't I doing it, what's wrong with me, I'm not a bloody invalid! So I have to go out. And now I'm desperately trying to think of reasons to go out and the fact is, I don't want to go out some days. And it's not like the year 1900 when I would possibly have been saving this woman from a terrible living on the streets. This doesn't put the bread in her mouth, this isn't her driving passion, she's at college, so I don't feel guilty about saying, "We don't want you any more." Basically, I think if I was sitting watching this programme and I was listening to myself going on and on about women's rights and

Above: *Paul, Joyce and Ruth in Greenwich Park, which was just over a mile from 50 Elliscombe Road. The family would go for a promenade in the park most weekends.*

liberation and stuff like that and then I ended up with a maid, it's like, "I *beg* your pardon, what the hell are you talking about?"

'It's also a personal thing. Like the other day we went for a walk together. She should have been cleaning and I should have been doing middle-class things, so what did we do, we went to Charlton Park and then we wandered round the graveyard and looked at some headstones, and then at some horses in the riding school there. And I was thinking, "This is bloody ridiculous, I can't go for a walk with my maid." I mean in the modern world there is no class distinction, but I doubt if a 1900 mistress of the house would have gone for a walk with her maid.

'And then there's the thing of it being half-past nine and she's not here and I suddenly turn into this horrible employer figure. Or, you know, on the day she mangled all the buttons off the shirts, which I thought was quite funny really, but then it was me that had to sit and sew them all on again.

'So what I'm trying to say is, I'm going to liberate Elizabeth. I'm setting her off free into the world to find her way and do her own thing. It's nothing personal, but I just can't have someone else coming in and cleaning up my house.'

It wasn't till the following Friday, however, that Joyce managed to write the letter that would be sent to Elizabeth; she didn't want to hurt her employee's feelings, or make her think she didn't like her or that she wasn't a good cleaner, and the letter itself said as much. Nonetheless liberation didn't feel the same from the ex-maid-of-all-work's perspective. 'I was stunned,' she wrote in her diary that evening. 'The reason she said was that she cannot get used to having me clean the house while she does nothing. That is exactly the problem – she does nothing. The times when she has been really miserable and I've spent hours cheering her up and this is the thanks I get from it. If she had any incentive to have a hobby she wouldn't be in my way, but she never goes out.

'I am so interested to see how she handles cleaning the house. In my opinion they will not clean the house for the next two weeks till they go home. I am very upset and feel very used. They waited until I had the house spotless before they let me go. I never worked so hard as what I did in that house and I found it so interesting as if I was in my great-grandmother's shoes. On Friday I polished six pairs of boots and scrubbed the

Cycling

Cycling was the great craze of the late nineteenth century. By the end of the century there were over 600,000 cycles in use in Britain. The Cycling Touring Club had 20,000 members, the National Cyclists' Union only slightly fewer, and each had its own monthly magazine. Cycling provided both exercise and diversion. For young women it also brought a degree of freedom and the chance to escape their chaperones. In 1900 the cycling world was evenly divided between tricyclists and bicyclists. It was generally allowed that women might ride tricycles, but there was growing alarm at their enthusiasm for bicycling. This 'movement', according to British sources at least, began in America, 'where the roads are very bad, and when tricycles were far too heavy'.

It was acknowledged that 'the seat and appearance of a lady' on a bicycle were 'precisely the same as on the other machine'; but 'seat and appearance' were not the only considerations. A fall, it was argued, 'is very likely some time or other, and those who have once seen a lady fall from such a machine will probably feel that it is unsuitable for her'.

Many women, however, were less squeamish on this point. And bicycle manufacturers were not slow to cater to their wants. 'Ladies' bicycles', with modified crossbars to make room for their skirts, soon became popular. Despite this arrangement it was still only too possible for female riders to get their skirts 'wound up' in the driving chain. The radical adoption of trousers and divided skirts did something to avert such disasters. Bicycles themselves were also becoming safer throughout the period. The 'dress guard' became more effective. There was a move to reduce the size of bicycle wheels and the weight (but not the strength) of the frames. Improvements in suspension led to a special 'anti-vibration' range, thought to be particularly suitable for women and 'delicate people'.

The new so-called 'safety machines' received glowing recommendations for their versatility and convenience. 'Indeed, with one of these a cyclist can go almost anywhere. He can get through a hedge easily; and a ploughed field, or even a fordable river, form no obstruction when the cycle is so light that it can be carried in one hand. Such machines are also very easily stowed away – in a passage, or anywhere.'

whole of the top floor including the windows. I admit I had a good cry about being dismissed. It's the first time I have ever been let go from a job and it's not a nice feeling at all. Kathryn the second oldest girl told me she would have gone mad at times if I hadn't been there to laugh and joke with her. I feel really let down and for the first time since I started at the house I feel like I'm working class and they are not.'

Above: *Joyce on the bicycle she was given towards the end of the experiment. She found it a great boon, enabling her to get out to Blackheath and Greenwich Park as well as to the shops. After this picture was taken she managed to find a hat pin, enabling her to cycle in her hat which would have been considered essential in 1900, and therefore put her shopping in her basket.*

Back to the Future

The day after she had written the letter that ended Elizabeth's tenure in the world of 1900, Joyce stayed in bed till 4 p.m. 'I just couldn't be bothered to get up,' she wrote in her diary. 'Paul brought me breakfast in bed (boiled eggs) and after that I just stayed here. My first day without having to get done up like an old woman. My nightie is preferable.'

She was reading Wilkie Collins's *Woman in White*. 'Didn't some Victorians lead pointless, BORING lives,' she wrote. 'I'm up to page 331. Laura Fairlie is a drip and Miss Halcombe needs to get a life. I have little sympathy for either of them at this point – come on, Wilkie, liven it up a bit. At the moment I'm rooting for the baddie.

'Women at this point in history were their own worst enemies. It must have been quite difficult to show guts or bravery – then you discover that droopy-drawers Lady Glyde can't even dress herself for dinner without Fanny her maid! Will she starve? Will she put her skirt on back to front? Will the reader get up and go to the pub? I'm sorry but menacing and scary it is not. The only scary thing so far seems to be Miss Halcombe's face.

'Does this make me an ignorant, insensitive philistine of a reader? No, from a (sort of) Victorian viewpoint I suddenly see how DULL + POINTLESS life was for so many of them. This book passes for the "greatest sensation" novel according to the blurb. Not from where I'm sitting (or rather lying) it doesn't.'

By four she had finished. 'Quite a clever piece,' she admitted. 'But not destined to be on my favourites list.'

'Who's been sleeping in our beds?'

Two weeks later the Bowlers would be moving out of the 1900 House. 'The time for leaving is getting nearer and nearer,' wrote Paul in his diary. 'My thoughts and everyone else's are on the final few days. I am not sure whether I will miss the year 1900. My life here has been enjoyable, but sometimes downright depressing. You have to find the right amount of time and energy to achieve a normal day. Even writing a diary or talking to the video

Above: *Hilary and Ruth with cockerel Charlie and hen Mason. Sadly, in the last week, Mason passed away, a very upsetting incident for all the family.*

camera takes a lot of energy.'

'I'm so familiar with my new life,' Joyce wrote. 'I'm not looking forward to returning to the old one.' Nonetheless, her imagination was already racing ahead to the departure. 'I've had lots of thoughts about how we leave on the last day.

'As I see the clothes as the time-travel device I'd like our modern clothes delivered here in brown paper parcels, so that we can take them upstairs, get changed, leave our old clothes on our beds and just leave. Just as we walked into our Victorian life, so I'd like to walk out, as if the real 1900 family could then resume their lives here; as if time hasn't moved for them but in that space we have spent three months here. I know this isn't a real 1900 home but wouldn't it be good if it was. I can imagine the family of 1900 coming back and saying, "Who's been sleeping in our beds? Who's been eating our porridge? Who's been breaking our chairs?" – because we have done all those things. What else will they say? "Who's been building a shed in our garden? Who put these chickens here? Who moved the postcard from Auntie Maud?"

It will be a very sad day when we go and I hope that the house will not feel too lonely or forlorn. I shall say thank you to the rooms and the things in them for making my experience so real. I am scared to leave now. I don't want it to end yet. What am I saying?!!! Oh Lord, I think I like it here! No, not "like", but it's familiar now.

'Paul has been lazy and not writing much of a diary,' she added, 'so I've written this, as we talked about it. Paul says: "We were a strong family, then within a week it dissolved, then we rebuilt it and we are stronger. Now we have a clearer understanding of who everyone is." I agree.'

'Since I've been here,' Ruth told her video diary, 'I've found out where everything is and where everything goes and what I do and everything and it just feels like home to me. But I must admit this wallpaper is a bit tacky.

'It's been really fun here and I have enjoyed a lot of it. I love the chickens. I really think I'll miss this place afterwards. We've read a lot while we've been here. I also enjoy talking to my doll Adele, because I can tell her secrets and things, and I'll be glad to take her home. She'll have pride of position in my bedroom, she'll be a reminder of this house.'

'I will definitely cry when I leave this place,' Hilary agreed, 'because I don't really want to go. I mean some people would just hate to live without electricity, and things like that, but I think it's really good. It teaches you about the things that you have and what you need. I mean this afternoon when I came back from school I desperately needed a glass of milk, but it's been warm so it was off, which shows what fridges are used for. It's really good, things like that.'

'1900 Journal'

The twins had decided to spend the last fortnight in the house writing a magazine. Partly to remember their experience, partly because they thought Joyce was bored with reading the 1900 *Illustrated London News*, and partly because they just wanted to. Miss H. Bowler was the Editor and Miss R. Bowler, with her faithful Box Brownie, the Photographer. She already had a number of pictures of the family in 1900 attitudes: Mummy on a bike, Mummy and Daddy, Dad by the shed he was building – known to the family as 'the Millennium shed' – and so on. Now, in addition to photo-bylines of Editor and Photographer, prominently displayed by the masthead of the *1900 Journal*, there were snaps of the family's recent trip to the Player's Theatre in Charing Cross, where they had seen *Ridgeway's Late Joys*, a Victorian music hall variety show. The play, Hilary said, had been 'really good' and the meal in the restaurant 'top class'. This part of the experience was encapsulated in a Restaurant Review on Page Two:

MENU
Starter: Melon
Main course: Roast Leg of Lamb
Dessert: Mixed Sorbet
Review:
The food was so delicious and the atmosphere was fun and lively. Service

1900 Journal

Photographer Miss K. Bowler
Editor Miss H. Bowler

[May 1900]   Issue 1   [Price Tuppence]

CONTENTS

VOTES FOR WOMEN ?

There have been rumours that women have been coming more open about there say in the VOTE!

We talked to Joyce Bowler about what she thinks women will achieve by this protest, she said: I feel the universal suffrage is long over due!

If a man can have the vote, I see no reason why a women can't. Women are not second class citizens.

I admit there is good and bad in men and women but just because a man is a man does not make him superior just for that.

I am very gratefull to my husband to my husband for his support in my campain to forward the cause of womens rights in society. I urge men and women to condsider carefully the future of our great nation and recognise the valuble role women can play.

I hope you condsider Mrs Bowlers debate on this campain.

reported by H. Bowler.

Above: *The front cover of the twins' 1900 Journal.*
Portraits of the Photographer and Editor are on either
side of the distinctive masthead.

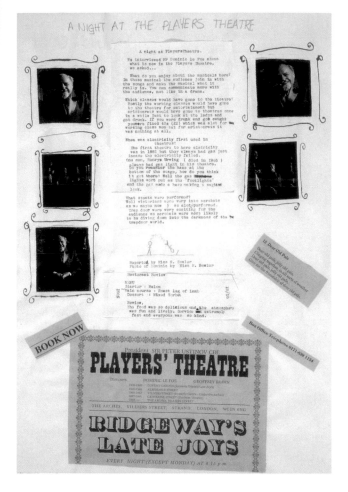

Above: *Page Two of the* 1900 Journal *features a review of a music hall night at the Player's Theatre in Charing Cross.*

Opposite: *The* Journal's *fashion centre spread made prominent use of a single late-Victorian model, Miss Kathryn Bowler.*

extremely fast and everyone was so kind. 10/10.

Alongside, by the feature article by Reporter Miss H. Bowler entitled 'A Night at the Player's Theatre', were no fewer than five portrait studies by Photographer Miss R. Bowler of Mr Dominic Le Foe, the Chairman of the Players' Theatre.

'Inside the magazine,' Ruth had told her video diary, 'we are going to have fashion, we've got loads of pictures of Kathryn, it's going to be excellent, like a remembrance thing for us, so we can remember being here and things.'

Besides the promised fashion spread ('the latest in dressing gowns, "just for the outdoors", Miss Kathryn declares') there was a page devoted to Agony Aunt 'Mrs Joyce'. 'Dear Mrs Joyce,' ran a typical letter, 'I am having problems with my twin sister. She is always copying what I do. She is really annoying and always in my way. Please help me and reply soon, Ruth.' Mrs Joyce's advice to this problem, as to letters from Miss Kathryn Bowler 'bemoaning the restrictions of her corset' and worrying about a 'corpulent' bottom, was simply to 'set off to the next meeting of the local branch of the Women's Social and Political Union'. 'Let us pray,' Mrs Joyce elaborated to Miss Kathryn, 'that the women of the future cast off their restrictions, both physical and mental, and do not have to wear corsets and do have the right to vote.' Her advice to 'Hilary', who complained of a youth who had tried to kiss 'her friend', was simple. 'You say that he follows you everywhere. Well dear, go to the local meeting of the WSPU – once he has followed you there he can open his eyes to the cause of women's rights…'

Other pages included a report of a family outing to the Victoria and Albert Museum, a Recipe Corner ('Beans, Potted'), Things in Season – May, Tips by Mr Paul Bowler on How to Build a Shed, and 'Mystic Ruth' who foresaw 'a new way of communicating with people in other countries', that 'the motor-car will be adapted to many wonderful styles and colours', and most tellingly of all, 'a dome will be built in Greenwich for the year 2000'.

1900 Fashion

Miss Kathryn Bowler has agreed to let us take some photographs of her in the latest '1900' fashion!

In this photograph Miss Bowler is standing next to her bicycle in a

lovely cream dress with blue flowers on it. It has a corset like front which is to be laced up with → string.

Here Miss Kathryn is getting ready to dive away in a lovely blue twopiece swimming costume with white patterns closed at the front with a sailor top collar! ↓

In this photograph Kathryn is showing us the latest underwear the corset a wonderful white colour and a wonderful 2 in 1 underwear special. "This is very un- comfortable!" says Miss Kathryn! ↓

The lastest in dressing gowns, "just for the outdoors" miss kathryn declares

A thespian future?

While the twins busied themselves with their magazine, Joyce and Kathryn were preparing to return to the Players' Theatre, this time for an audition for the music hall. 'It's like saying,' Joyce confessed the night before, 'tomorrow I'm going to climb the Matterhorn, tomorrow I'm going to swim the Channel. I don't have the talent to climb or swim or do any of those things, and I'm equally poorly equipped to go on stage. I don't know if it qualifies as stage fright, but I get a funny sort of prickly feeling at the back of my legs when I think about it. Oh well, I'll give it a go. I'll get out there and give it what-for, I will feel terribly exposed standing up there on stage, it's a piece I've written so I'm open to criticism, it's going to be delivered and sung by myself and Kathryn; all right I can't sing, but it's a bit of fun, it doesn't matter if it's awful, it isn't the way I earn my living, yet something inside me secretly wants to do it, does that make sense, am I mad? Oh well, by this time tomorrow it will all be over, or not, as the case may be.'

Kathryn, too, was 'a little bit scared' about the audition. 'No, I'm not,' she added to her video diary, 'I'm extremely frightened, I haven't been on the stage for ages, I mean I do Performing Arts at college and we perform all the time, but not on a proper stage. I've got so much adrenaline rushing through my whole body and I'm scared for Mum as well. The fact is she's never been on stage before, and she's got to do so much more than me. I just have to stand there and sort of prance about a bit, but Mum really has to concentrate on what she's saying and how she's doing it.'

'Secretly,' Joyce confessed in her written diary, 'I do have thespian ambitions, but I always feel that I'd never cut the mustard. There are plenty of second-rate actors out there – why swell the ranks?'

'I'm extremely glad it's over,' she told her video diary the next day. 'I did enjoy it, it was very strange, because before I was terrified of going on the stage, but it wasn't scary at all really. The nerves I'd had all day just went, I didn't feel nervous at all, in fact I felt I really enjoyed it. I don't know what I was worried about, I just got up there and felt great, perhaps because it was a small stage, I don't know, I could have done it again. Dominic was particularly polite in calling our act "interesting", which was obviously code for something else.'

'I just suddenly thought,' she added a little later, 'my God we must have been so bad. The thought of me stood up there belting out tuneless, enormously loud, bellowing. I mean, that poor man Dominic Le Foe must have felt like he was being attacked by a load of female walruses. I felt quite pleased with myself this morning, but I think that that was just because I'd

The spiritual life

The late-Victorian period is generally regarded as an age of declining faith and growing secularisation. It was a view that was common even at the time. Certainly advances in science did seem to undermine some of the supposed certainties of religious faith, while the increased involvement of the state in matters of social welfare reduced the traditional role of the church in this area.

Nevertheless there were significant currents running against this general trend. Anglican church attendance, especially among the middle classes, actually increased during the year around 1900, although whether it was undertaken as a social duty rather than a spiritual need is difficult to determine. Many people were looking outside the established church to assuage their spiritual needs. It was perhaps as an extreme reaction against the universal claims of modern science that spiritualism became so popular during this period. Ouija boards enjoyed a vogue. And even the cautious, church-going Mr Pooter of Diary of a Nobody found himself drawn into a séance.

actually done it. Now I'm thinking, "Oh my God, I'm surprised I had the gall to show my face with them afterwards." I hope it isn't excruciatingly painful to watch.'

Paul meanwhile, had started to think about the altogether larger performance to which the family had committed themselves. 'I am starting to worry,' he wrote in his diary, 'about how it will all come out. What will be cut and what will they use. We are a normal family doing something extraordinary. TV can and will make things the way they wish to.' Joyce had been speculating along similar lines. 'Thinking about what will and won't be used for the programme, I feel very sensitive about it. Would an artist paint a picture, then give a big pair of scissors to someone and say, "Cut out the bits you want to keep"? That's what it feels like to us. All our work is being reviewed, cut, changed, put in and out of sequence and manipulated. But this isn't just our work – it's OUR LIVES.'

Kathryn's seventeenth birthday came and went, with cake, cards, presents and an authentic magic-lantern show of *Alice in Wonderland* put on by neighbours Fred and Ruth, on a machine that had been in Fred's family since the last century. 'A wonderful Victorian birthday,' Kathryn called it.

Mason died, leaving Fortnum and Patricia alone with the cockerel Charlie, a sad event which upset all members of the family and earnt the deceased bird an obituary in the *1900 Journal*.

> OBITUARY.
>
> MASON
> A fine chicken.
> Sadly missed by
> us all.
>
> Thankyou for being our chicken.

Above: *Mason's obituary in the 1900 Journal.*

Life will never be the same

All of a sudden the family were into the last week. 'It feels very strange,' Joyce said, 'it's a slight sort of holiday feeling, like suppressed hysteria really this morning, but tinged with sadness because we've all got really mixed feelings about going back. Even Joe, who says he's fed up with being Victorian and wants to go back to being himself, hasn't quite grasped that we won't be taking everything with us and that it won't be quite the same the week after next.

'I think we've spent three months creating new identities for ourselves and forming ourselves into people that can live here. I think we've become the 1900 House family and now it's going to be really hard to go back to being ourselves again, within twenty-four hours, if not quicker. They're all going back to school and back to work within the space of a few days. Will it take me three months to learn how to be who I was before? Certainly life will never be the

Above: *Paul making toast at the kitchen range, which was much faster than normal electric toasters, browning the bread 'literally in seconds'. Paul took charge of breakfast every day, rising earliest to boil water for tea, then making porridge and toast as the family emerged one by one.*

same for any of us – who knows, I could go into panto. D'you think they'd have me?'

'All my thoughts are on the next few days,' wrote Paul. 'How am I going to revert? How are the children and Joyce going to revert? I want to support them in their final few days. It is good that the children are going to school, to ensure their thoughts are not fully focused on the last few days here.'

'I feel like I don't know how to be 1999 Joyce any more,' Joyce wrote in her diary. 'We seem to have slowed down so enormously. Even down to how long it takes to boil a kettle for tea, and having the patience to wait. Paul thinks he's become more deliberate and clear thinking as a result. From a hyper-hyper workaholic that's something.'

Joyce sat at the front window of the 1900 House, looking out for the last time as her 1900 self on to 1999. 'I like to sit here and see what's happening in the street,' she confided. 'You get a good view up and down Elliscombe Road. I like to look at the tree outside and see how it's gone from being very sticky and twiggy to having buds on it and little leaves and now you

can see the sycamore keys growing on it and the leaves are big.

'In the great scheme of things being in this house, doing this experiment for three months, is small beer, isn't it? It's not exactly going to change the future of our country, I can't see it radically influencing anything. Maybe it might spark some interest in somebody to discover their own family history. What I'm trying to say is for three months it has overpowered me, eaten me up and absorbed me, and now I see that I must come back to reality, come back to being who I am.'

Above: *The larder. Without a fridge, Joyce quickly learned to buy perishable goods in very small amounts. True to the period, milk was delivered twice a day and Joyce kept it in the cooler scullery.*

Leaving

To round off the experience it had been decided that the Bowlers would give a party, to thank many of the people who had been involved with the project from the start. So the little garden was crowded with not just the Bowlers, but Daru Rooke the historian; the two local doctors, Dr John and Dr Jo; the baker Terry; Fred Hams the chicken expert; Peter Riddington the architect; Chris Ridley the stills photographer; neighbours Fred and Ruth, Nick and Lynn, Tracy and Trevor; Pam, a work colleague of Joyce's; Natalie, her childhood friend, with husband Paul and children; Joyce's sister Katrina; not to mention all the stalwarts of the

Photography

Although the principles of photographic reproduction were established in the late 1830s, it was not until the last decades of the nineteenth century that photography developed into a widespread hobby. The innovation which led to this development was the work of George Eastman, an American inventor. In 1880 he perfected a method of making dry photographic plates, which could be easily kept and used when convenient. Previously photographers had had to coat their own plates as they needed them – a laborious and not-uncomplicated business.

Four years later he dispensed with the need for individual photographic plates by inventing the first 'roll film'. It was so sensitive that pictures could be taken 'instantaneously' without any awkward wait.

In 1888 Eastman began marketing the Kodak camera (the name 'Kodak' was another of his inventions). The early Kodak models came ready-loaded with a hundred exposures; after the film had been shot, the camera was sent back to the factory for development and re-loading. Further refinements to the system, however, soon allowed the amateur either to send just the film back to the factory or to develop it at home.

Photography was often regarded as an adjunct to other hobbies, rather than as an art in its own right. As Cassell's noted, 'The person who goes in for natural-history specimens, and walks a deal, will often wish he could take a picture of the lovely scenes he comes in view of. He may or may not be an artist, but photography is always open to everyone… In a family of which one member adopts photography as a hobby, beautiful landscapes may be taken as lantern transparencies, which some clever sister can easily colour, to be used as slides by another brother, whose pet amusement is the magic lantern.'

1900 saw the introduction of Eastman's simplest camera yet: the Box Brownie. It was easy to use, inexpensive and ideal for children. Photography was put within the reach of all.

Wall To Wall TV team. There were sandwiches and cheese straws and cakes and sausage rolls and tea and lemonade and ginger beer and two authentic 1900 punches – a Pimm's and a strawberry punch. The sun shone and the highlight of the afternoon was The Grand Opening of Paul's 'Millennium Shed', a more useful construction, Joyce thought, than the Millennium Dome down the road.

That evening the sky darkened in a thunderstorm. 'Extremely fitting,' observed Joyce, as she stood by her bedroom window in a nightie. 'I don't want to go home, I want to stay here. Just when I start to get it right, to know what I'm doing here, I have to go home.'

She had had the last bath she would ever have in the house, read Joe the last bedtime story. Fred Hams had taken the chickens back, and in the morning there would be no cock-a-doodle-doo at dawn. 'It's so sad,' she said. 'Unfortunately 1900 has become so real to us, in a short space of time, that I think it's going to be really hard to give it up. Tomorrow is going to be extremely difficult.'

In the morning she clipped on her corset for the last time. 'I'm actually having trouble remembering what my other clothes look like and what I wear every day,' she said. True to her wishes they were to arrive in brown paper parcels.

Paul had shaved off his moustache. 'I've grown it for just over two months,' he observed. 'It was part of my time-travel, and that part has now gone. Clothes should be arriving soon, I think, and then once I get my clothes on, I would like to walk out the door and not come back. Everyone is laughing, but inside, I think everyone is sad. Joyce and I are certainly very sad to leave this house and the year 1900. We've created our own little world here, for better or worse, and it's been a privilege. People have said, "Would you continue?" and sometimes I have said, "No, there's no way I could stand it," but today I could stay forever, recollecting things I've done, places we've been, mementoes that have been sat on shelves, and it's really quite weird. We've moved lots and lots of times in our lives, so it shouldn't be that hard to go, but this time it really is. Thank you very much for a wonderful privileged look at the year 1900.'

'We're leaving soon,' said Hilary, ' which is sad because I feel that we live here and this is our house now. We've got into a routine that can't be broken unless we time-travel, which is what we are going to do today. I'll really miss it here, it was so brilliant and it's just one of those

Above: *The Bowlers prepare to say goodbye. Just before they left, Chris Ridley, the photographer who had helped Paul and Ruth with their cameras, took a formal portrait of the family, in the Victorian style, using a plate camera of the period.*

things that we just want to keep forever. Dad has set out his clothes on the bed, for the next person; I'm going to do that with mine. First of all I didn't like it here and I wanted to go home, and then in the end I wanted to stay, I really don't want to go, it's just such a nice experience here.'

'The Bowlers have gone,' observed Jonathan Barker, one of the directors of the programmes, a little later, 'But their ghosts are still here, and although we've just come to get some shots of this and that, and the house is more of a film set now, it's still got a living being.'

Soon, though, even the house would be dismantled. Many of the props had been rented and would have to go back; the Victorian furniture would be sold, and 50 Elliscombe Road would return, like its occupants, to 1999. Only the film and diaries of those three latter-day months of 1900 would remain. And all the other secret ups and downs and highs and lows of the individuals of the Bowler family in their 1900 House would just be memories, fading fast.

Afterword
1999 Again

Joe

'Were you looking forward to coming back?'
'Yes.'
'Why?'
'So I can get on the computer.'
'Did you enjoy being in Victorian times?'
'No.'
'If your Mum and Dad said to you you're coming back to 1900 in six months, would you fancy coming?'
'No.'

Ruth

'We're back home and it's great because I've been on the computer, I've watched the telly, I've played my music and this afternoon I went on the phone to one of my friends to ask them if they could come round on Thursday. I've seen all my teddies and Adele has got pride of place in my bedroom as well. I like listening to the radio because it's got modern songs on and I'm going to go out, maybe tomorrow and buy them. And I'm going to have my ears pierced. This morning I just couldn't wait to have some chocolate cornflakes and cold milk. Hilary kept going, 'Oh, it's cold milk, it's *cold milk.*'

Hilary

'I bought a new CD and the music is just so loud, so lively, and it's really, really good. I bought an album and Ruth bought herself a single, so we've got like our favourite stuff. All we've been doing is listening to music and reading our *Point Horror* books and looking up Leonardo di Caprio and stuff. I do miss Elliscombe Road, it's really nice there and everybody knew each other, well sort of, but I think I feel better in my 1999 world than I did in my 1900, because I felt really strange and here we're normal again, I feel, I don't know, just better to be like this.'

Kathryn

'It's absolutely fantastic being back and I'm loving every minute of it. I've seen my friends and I've played my music and I've been out and bought lots of products and just been the old Kathryn Bowler again. I'm going out tonight on my first night out for three months and I'm really, really excited and I've just had a shower and washed my hair and now I'm going to blow dry it and put some gorgeous styling products on it and I'm going to put my make-up on and get ready, just pamper myself to the max and have a really nice time tonight, and I'm so looking forward to it, it's something that keeps me going and keeps me normal, just being able to go out with my mates and have a really good laugh – oh I can't wait.'

Joyce

'Right, I'm doing the washing up. What you do is, you stack it all in this big white box in the kitchen, and then you put a little powder in a receptacle and then you shut the door and push a button and it washes all the plates and cutlery up somehow and it's great. I've been totally bonkers since I came home. I've turned all the lights on and turned them off again, I've watched advertisements on television, I've made toast in the toaster, cups of tea, it's very strange. I've got an invisible fairy maid and she's called Electricity and she whizzes around the house doing everything for me.

'I just can't get over having an indoor toilet, and soft loo paper too. We bought the Sunday papers, but d'you know I just couldn't read them, I just flicked through them all. I just thought, "Overload". It was an overload of information, I don't think that I really needed any of it.

'Paul and I have been shopping at a well-known supermarket, spent a small fortune, it took us two hours just to restock the house. We bought things we'd forgotten even existed, there was so much choice, racks and racks of stuff, I haven't a clue what I'm going to do with half of it. You can buy a different cleaner for practically everything in the house, not to mention your face and hair.

'I actually felt quite lonely this evening. I missed everyone else that was involved in the whole experience, people knocking on the door and dropping by. Having the production team coming by so frequently did simulate in a way the life that a Victorian lady of the turn of the century might have had in her home, because I think you would have had a lot of social interactions with people in the street. And in the modern world, because we are all so busy, and because we go to work and so on, there isn't so much of that. We've had numerous telephone conversations with people today, but not real contact, not face to face, touching, looking, being close to, interrupting their body language, reading the signs on their face, there hasn't been much of that really.'

Paul

'Now that it's all ended, I personally would like to go back. Joyce agrees with me, we'd like to come back, please, in another year or so. Back here everyone has returned to 1999 and arguments are going, but they're upstairs, not down here, not what I would call in-your-face. They've got things to amuse themselves with upstairs: music, television, computers, a variety of food, so all their needs are extremely well catered for in 1999. Whereas in 1900 we were limited to conversation, emotional outbursts which had to be dealt with on the spot, and also with a restricted diet, and all those things combined could make you pretty grumpy, but it was a wonderful time and I feel like I've lost something. I miss the people, I miss the baker, I miss going to Charlie's for the groceries, getting to know him so well. Whereas now we go to the big supermarket, and they try and portray it as personal, but it's not, it's impersonal. Perhaps in parts of the country there are still the bakers and butchers and grocers that people go to and know really well, but not here. We've known that at Elliscombe Road and we miss it terribly.'

Above: *Paul was sorry when his three months as a 'time-traveller' came to an end. Both he and Joyce missed their 1900 life once they got home to Somerset.*

Suppliers Index

Antiques

Tsar Fireplaces
487 Liverpool Road
London N7 8PG
Tel: 0171 609 4238
Fax: 0171 609 1883

The Old Cinema
157 Tower Bridge Road
London SE1 3LW
Tel: 0171 407 5371
Fax: 0171 403 0359
Email: theoldcinema@antiques-
uk.co.uk

Architectural Salvage

Restoration
33a Avenue Road
Norwich
Norfolk NR2 3TH
Tel: 01603 441096

Brondersbury Salvage
The Yard
136 Willesden Lane
London NW6 7TE
Tel: 0171 328 0820
Fax: 0171 328 0280

Children's books

Ripping Yarns
355 Archway Road
London N6 4EJ
Tel: 0181 341 6111
Fax: 0171 482 5056
Email: yarns@easynet.co.uk

Curtains

Anna French
343 Kings Road
London SW3 5ES
Tel: 0171 351 1126
Fax: 0171 351 0421

Ironmongery

Franchi Locks and Tools
279 Holloway Road
London N7 6NE
Tel: 0171 607 2200
Fax: 0171 700 4050
Email: info@franchi.co.uk

Kitchenalia

Sara Lemkow
12 Camden Passage
London N1 8AD
Tel: 0171 359 0190
Fax: 0171 704 2095
Email: saralembow@btinternet.com

Kathryn Cureton
9 Bolingbroke Grove
London SW11 6ER
Tel: 0181 673 3608

Lighting

Sugg Gas Lighting
Sussex Manor Business Park
Gatwick Road
Crawley
West Sussex RH10 2GD
Tel: 01293 540111
Fax: 01293 540114
Email: sales@sugglighting.co.uk

Christopher Wray Lighting
591–593 Kings Road
London SW6 2YW
Tel: 0171 736 8434
Fax: 0171 731 3507
Email: sales@christopher-wray.com

Linen

Bryony Thomasson
19 Ackmar Road
London SW6 4UP
Tel: 0171 731 3693
(by appointment only)

Piano

Pianorama
47 Westfield Road
Leeds
West Yorkshire LS3 1DD
Tel/Fax: 0113 244 5143
Email: colin@pianorama.co.uk

Range

O'Neill's Antiques
190 Kettering Road
Northampton
Northamptonshire NN1 4BJ
Tel/Fax: 01604 603664

Toys

Hawking Bazaar
St Margaret Harleston
Norfolk IP20 0PJ
Tel: 01986 782536
Fax: 01986 782468
Email: hawking@ukonline.co.uk

Wallpapers

Watts of Westminster
2/9 Chelsea Harbour Design Centre
London SW10 0XE
Tel: 0171 376 4486
Fax: 0171 376 4636
Email: wattsofwestminster@iddv.com

Cole and Son
G/9 Chelsea Harbour Design Centre
London SW10 0XE
Tel: 0171 376 7578
Fax: 0171 376 4631

Alexander Beauchamp
Greenacremill
Fireholm Lane
Stacksteads
Bacup
Lancashire OL13 0EZ
Tel: 01706 872155
Fax: 01706 872156

Index

Acknowledgements

Mark McCrum would like to thank the Bowler family for cups of tea and always friendly cooperation; Simon Shaw and the team at Wall To Wall for creative input and detail-chasing; Matthew Sturgis for being the perfect collaborator; Emma Tait, editor at Channel 4 Books, for holding it all together; and Leonie Edward-Jones for general support at home.

Matthew Sturgis would like to thank Daru Rooke, Katy Butler, Peter Riddington, George Cox, Lia Cramer, Simon Shaw, and all the Wall To Wall team for being so generous with their knowledge and time.

Wall To Wall would like to thank the following people:
For renovation and restoration work: Daru Rooke, Dr Evelyn Silber, Leeds Museums and Art Galleries, Peter Riddington the architect, Donald Insall Associates, Derek Ednie, Martin Thorpe, George Cox, Roger Monk and all the members of the renovation team from Holloway, White, Allom. Also, Katy Butler the horticultural historian, Henry Doubleday Research Association and Mike Bishop of the The Heating and Plumbing Company.

For period materials: Lia Cramer the art director and her assistant Nick Scott, Rosalind Ebbut the period costume designer, Jane McDonagh at Cosprops, Tony Hellard at Angels and Bermans and Christine Walmsley-Cotham for hair and make-up.

For historical research: Clive Wainwright at the The Victoria and Albert Museum, Peter Brears the food historian, Dr John Hunt the pharmaceutical historian, Fred Hams the poultry historian, Pam Sambrooke from Keele University, Matthew Scott for his assistance with music in the house, Chris Ridley for photography advise, The Museum of London, Diana Dollery, The Fawcett Library, Woodlands Local History Library in Greenwich, The London Players Theatre and Mike Stanesby, Jane Owen and Carole Owen-Lord at the Shugborough Estate.

They would also like to thank the following suppliers: Terry Ayres at Ayres Bakery in Eltham, Charlie Judd of Apples and Oranges in Charlton, Martin Barry of Mel Family Butchers in Charlton, the Co-op in Charlton village, Dairycrest Dairies and Trumpers of Mayfair.

Thanks also to Jaime Brassard, Emile Bradshaw and Amanda Swanne who did work experience for the programme.

Finally thanks to Lieutenant-Colonel G. Ebbut and Major K. De Val of the Royal Marines, Mathew Little of the Royal Marines Corps Museum, Chris Bruton and Susan Bush at Fossdene Primary School, Ms Fulton at St Ursula's Convent School, Bryony Ford at Christ the King Sixth Form College, Greenwich Council Film Office and the residents of Elliscombe Road, especially Dr Joanna Long and Ruth and Fred.

Special thanks to Sara Ramsden at Channel 4.

Picture credits

Chris Ridley © Chris Ridley/Channel 4/Channel 4 Books: 2 (all pictures), 7, 8, 9, 10, 46, 47 (both pictures), 48, 51, 52, 53, 54 (all pictures), 56 (both pictures), 57, 58, 59 (both pictures), 60, 61, 62, 63, 64, 65, 66, 67, 68, 69 (both pictures), 70 (both pictures), 71 (all pictures), 72, 73t, 74, 75, 77 (all pictures), 78, 80, 81, 82, 83, 84, 88, 92, 94, 95, 97, 99, 101, 103, 105, 107, 108, 109, 111, 114, 116, 117, 119, 121, 123, 128, 130, 131, 133, 135, 136, 145, 148, 149, 150 (both pictures), 158, 159, 161, 162, 163, 164, 166, 170, 171 (both pictures), 173, 175, 182, 183, 185, 188. Hilary Bowler: 129. Joseph Bowler: 100, 137. Paul Bowler: 151, 156. Ruth and Hilary Bowler: 177, 178, 179, 181. Cassell's *Book of the Household* 1900: 134, 142, 157. Dover Images: 1. E.T. Archive: 18 (F.L.M. Forster/London Museum), 24 (Max Beerbohm/Garrick Club), 29t. Greenwich Local History Library: 13, 28, 32t. Hulton Getty: 19, 21b, 22b, 23, 27t, 30b, 37 (both pictures), 43. Mary Evans Picture Library: 15 (*Illustrated London News*), 17 (*Penny Illustrated*), 20 (*Chatterbox*), 21t (*Living London*), 22t, 25 (*Living London*), 26 (Ernest Prater/*Sporting Pictures*), 29b, 30t (*The Queen's London*), 31 (J Williamson/*Peeps at France*), 36t, 38, 40t (H.C. Sepping-Wright), 40b. *Punch*: 16, 27b, 32b, 33, 36b, 73b, 79, 118.